DARK PRAYER

DARK PRAYER

When all words fail...

❖❖❖❖❖❖❖❖❖❖❖❖❖❖❖❖❖❖❖❖❖❖

Letters to travellers

by

DAVID WOOD

CAIRNS PUBLICATIONS

HARLECH

2004

© David Wood, 2004

All rights reserved.

British Library Cataloguing in Publication Data

A record for this book is available from the British Library

ISBN 1 870652 42 8

CAIRNS PUBLICATIONS
Dwylan, Stryd Fawr, Harlech, Gwynedd LL46 2YA

www.cottercairns.co.uk
office@cottercairns.co.uk

Typeset in Monotype Baskerville by
Strathmore Publishing Services, London EC1

Printed in Great Britain by
Biddles Ltd, Kings Lynn

CONTENTS

PREFACE

When all words fail: it is a place we all come to, not once, but again and again. It is a lonely place, and we think we are alone. But we are in fact in good company. It is not a place to be afraid of, but one of necessary solitude where, ultimately, we meet everybody else. It may feel like a place of failure, where we have fallen off the edge of the world. But in the end it is not a place to be afraid of, but one we have to come to if we are to grow up and into the life we were made for.

In the early 1980s I went on a three-month pilgrimage through monastic communities in France, Belgium, Germany, and Holland. I had been pursuing silence for many years in retreats and workshops, but on this occasion I was exploring the title of one of Thomas Merton's books, *Contemplation in a World of Action*. I wanted to see if and how contemplative practice and the descent into silence could make fit with an active life.

The places and people and meetings remain vivid in my memory. They marked me for ever. But at the same time I was in deep trouble. I was running away from the challenges of intimacy at home, and so running away from my real self. I was living a split and thinking I could get away with it.

I came home to a new job, the care of a semi-rural parish smaller than the one I had been working in, so that I would have more time both to pray and to help others to pray, particularly in connection with Lindisfarne, Holy Island, off the coast of Northumberland. But this was no solution: my personal, working, active life was miles apart from my so-called spiritual life. Whilst I was leading others in exciting spiritual exercises, my own inner journey was on a downward spiral, out of control. As my daughter sharply observed one day, "How is it, Dad, that all this prayer doesn't make any difference to the way you are at home?"

It was the old, old story, which has been repeated again and again, of being enmeshed in the thrills and spills of glamorous spiritual adventuring with those who were attracted to it and to me. I had been pulled up short. What could I do?

Mercifully, the Holy Spirit who dwells within us does not withdraw from us, whatever mess we have got ourselves into. The grace, the gifts, the promises remain. Two lines haunted me from my sabbatical: "You did not choose me, but I chose you, and I commissioned you to go out and bear fruit, fruit that will last." (John 15.6) And the question: "What will you offer for the peace of the world?"

I felt helpless before the question. Who? Me? What can I do? Then it came to me. Why not pray the 'three hours' every Friday? What more helpless, useless thing could I do? Now Good Friday had always been important for me and at some point it had become every Friday. I could not pass Friday by; every week I had to stop and look at it. But to pray those hours from noon until three? Every Friday? I have to say that the notion came to me as a gift, and subsequent practice, however inadequate, has proved it to be perhaps the most extravagant gift I have ever been given, though I have no words to describe it.

As I started to do this, the rest of my life went on. I had to leave the parish I had recently arrived in and start all over again in a different part of the country. Relationships were broken and I had to start learning the meaning of 'love' all over again, right at the 'a' of the alphabet. Maybe nothing is lost, but such dead ends and new beginnings are bewildering, even staggering. I was taken on with trust and friendship, and life has become richer than ever before.

Mine is a traveller's tale, nothing more. We are all brilliant and awful at the same time, a tension we have to live, arms outstretched, until our last breath. Some have had to struggle with the conceits and despairs of the ego at deeper levels of darkness than mine, in terrifying washed-out places of desolation.

So it was that a year after starting to pray the 'three hours' I started to write these letters, and I have been cheered on by enough people to continue into the present. Little by little others have joined me in their own ways, in their solitude in different parts of the country. The letters are meant for your encouragement, and not least that you be gentle with yourself. Use them slowly, as meditations to chew on, ruminated, one at a time. Perhaps a retreat in the midst of daily life, in a deliberate set-aside time. You will find that I repeat myself, partly because I'm getting a bit ancient, partly because good news and good stories are worth hearing more than once. May you discover a few signposts for your own journey.

And perhaps I shouldn't have been surprised by this, but a couple of years after I started, I discovered the Society of the Precious Blood at Burnham Abbey near Maidenhead in Berkshire, a community of Sisters who have been keeping the 'three hours' every day, usually in complete silence, for the last hundred years! One of them has commented, "It can be heavy, dry, a time of fighting sleepiness, but always it has its own authenticity, and none of us would want to miss it." And the intention of this silent offering is always for the peace of the world.

DAVID WOOD
Maryport, February 2004

FOREWORD

What has been a twice yearly letter for those who are on the mailing list of the Community of the Three Hours is now available for a wider readership. The more hidden experience, and rightly so, is that of a group of people who in their own way remember Jesus on the cross for the three hours he is traditionally assumed to have hung there for the salvation of the world. Both the letters and the hidden witness have made a unique contribution to the Church, and for that we should be truly grateful.

First then, let us look at the letters, which cover the years 1986–2004. They work on a grand scale in terms of subject matter, but each is rarely more than two sides of A4, and over the years they have remained resolutely personal. The most persistent theme is 'dark prayer'. The idea hangs loosely on the ancient tradition of the Church of experiencing the glory of God only through the darkness, or the cloud. The great texts for this are Moses' experience of the hidden God at Mount Sinai in Exodus chapters 33 and 34. Believers experience an entry into darkness, a cloud of unknowing which is a test of faith. Indeed, faith is the only bow that can fire a 'longing dart of love' into the darkness and receive rewards. References to this tradition of prayer are taken from *The Cloud of Unknowing*, Henry Vaughan's poems and Meister Eckhart's writings.

However, there is another sort of darkness described in these letters, and that is the darkness of the temporary loss of sight of Christ as he enters the deep and troubled places of the world, traditionally called 'the descent into hell'. It is the contemporary experiences of darkness that most impact in these letters: Nelson Mandela, Bosnia, the Shoah, the Twin Towers, and many others. The sharpest outburst is reserved for the film *Trainspotting*. The letters refuse to hide from the dark side of our society today, and although we may think we are in touch with such matters, to have them placed before us in the shadow of the crucifixion, is to allow creative outcomes at least to be acknowledged. Spiritual writers most frequently called upon to guide us in the darkness are Etty Hillesum, John Main, Anthony de Mello, and Alan Ecclestone.

We do not gather from these letters any visual or practical idea of how the Three Hours can be spent. There is no swapping of ideas of posture, venue, food intake, pictures to meditate on, or whether music is allowed. Waiting and silence are the key words. "This dark prayer is so simple, so poor, so still, with hardly a word, hardly a breath. And it feels worthless, useless. And yet it can console, not least when the emptiness is shared in the company of others." (Letter Eleven) The letters are what we can see and read. Behind the letters is a company of contemporary saints who keep watching and waiting in faith, however dark that may be. The rewards? God knows.

DAVID SCOTT
Winchester, January 2004

Do not give up working for peace. Always remember that the peace for which you work is not of this world. Do not let yourself be distracted by the great noises of war, the dramatic descriptions of misery, and the sensational expressions of human cruelty. The newspapers, films, and war novels may make you numb, but they do not create in you a true desire for peace. They tend to create feelings of shame, guilt, and powerlessness, and these feelings are the worst motives for peace work.

Keep your eyes on the prince of peace, the one who doesn't cling to his divine power, the one who refuses to turn stones into bread, jump from great heights, and rule with great power. See the one who touches the lame, the crippled, and the blind, the one who speaks words of forgiveness and encouragement, the one who dies alone, rejected, and despised. Keep your eyes on him who becomes poor with the poor, weak with the weak, and who is rejected with the rejected. That one, Jesus, is the source of all peace.

Where is his peace to be found? The answer is surprising but it is clear: in weakness. Few people are telling this truth, but there is peace to be found in our own weakness, in those places of the heart where we feel most broken, most insecure, most in agony, most afraid. Why there? Because in our weakness our familiar ways of controlling and manipulating our world are being stripped away and we are forced to let go from doing much, thinking much, and relying on our self-sufficiency. Right there where we are most vulnerable, the peace that is not of this world is mysteriously hidden.

HENRY NOUWEN
Finding My Way Home

THE COMMUNITY
OF THE THREE HOURS

THE INVITATION
1986

> At midday a darkness fell over the whole land
> which lasted until three in the afternoon.
>
> MARK 15.33, *Revised English Bible*

This is a call to prayer in silence with others. It is a call to choose
to wait helplessly with those in the world who have no choice but
to wait helplessly. It is a call to wait, to hold open with prayer the
gateway of the kingdom so that others may come in by the little
unseen miracles of your waiting love.

Who joins?

Ask yourself, Am I willing to offer this prayer for the peace of
the world?

If your answer is a simple, straightforward Yes, that in itself is
an act of deep commitment, whatever you decide in detail.

> "Whom shall I send? Who will go for us?"
> "Here am I: send me."
>
> ISAIAH 6.8

You then decide which sort of membership. There are some
people who will be able to offer the traditional 'Good Friday
Three Hours' every Friday from noon until 3 p.m., doing nothing
in that time except wait in prayer as Christ waited. It is both a lot
to ask and little to offer, in the light of how we often spend the
rest of our time. But there are also those who will wish to give the

I

three hours, but who cannot because of work or family commitments or simply because this is not something they are able to
do on their own. They might offer some 'waste' time during
the week, not necessarily on a Friday. But they would make a
sufficiently strong commitment to wish to be associated. Even to
make a recollection at some time between twelve and three on a
Friday would be solidarity enough.

A list of names and addresses can be circulated to those who
wish. It may help some to have a map of where others live.
    If people wish to gather with others who live near, that is up
to them. Most people will probably make their offering on their
own – as Christ did.
    Will you offer this for the peace of the world?

The invitation is still open

If you are interested in possibly joining the Community of the
Three Hours please contact David Wood at 6 John Street,
Maryport, Cumbria, CA15 6JT.

THE LETTERS

LETTER ONE
All Saintstide 1986

Many people know my family news and wonder where I am. Thanks. In my heart of hearts, beneath all the confusion and stuff that we all know about and there is no need to go into, this letter is where I am. It is my sense of direction. It has been growing in me for some years, becoming clearer and clearer.

I want to share it with you and invite your response.

Like most of us I feel helpless, a dead weight, when faced with the massive issues of justice and peace in the world. What can I do? The scale is so enormous. I am not even a drop in the bucket. What is the use? You know the territory.

On sabbatical in 1983 I first found myself hearing the question, Will you give your life for the peace of the world? Many have given their lives in war that peace may be restored. They risked everything. Did they throw their lives away? Was it a useless waste? We are in so-called peacetime in this country, but we know that this is not really the case. There have been a hundred or more wars since 1945, some of them major, and every war has mercifully become our war. It *is* an act of mercy: it could be the occasion of spiritual growth in the life of the world.

Will you give your life for the peace of the world?

We run away from our feelings of helplessness. It seems like the edge of doom: it is certainly a dark place. And it feels like failure: we should surely have done more. We want to feel useful, successful, contributing our little bit. But it doesn't seem to make much difference, and even the best of us run round in circles of aid and protest – not least in the churches. But to 'wait' feels worse. For in the waiting we have to face the feelings of helpless-ness. Worse, it can seem like paralysis.

I believe there is a call for some to choose to stay with this darkness, to wait around, stand around helplessly but in prayer. It is to do nothing, to face the nothing, the emptiness, to face the vast sense of loss and waste. Dare we spend time going into this darkness deliberately, utterly dependent on the mystery beyond and outside ourselves, to stay there, unable to move?

In choosing to do this we identify with something like half the world's population who have no choice but to wait. They spend most of their lives, day by monotonous day, waiting for justice, even for someone to move towards them with a gesture of mercy. The starving, the sick, the prisoners, the infants, the very old and the prematurely old: they are trapped. They have no choice. They live in an enormous outpatients' department, each waiting their turn. There is nothing to do except to wait.

To choose to identify with them as closely as we can is to allow the mystery of human suffering and rebirth to enter us. It is something of the mystery of God. It is to trust that prayer does change things and is the most subversive of all activities. It is to shift to a different level the offering of ourselves to work for peace and justice. It is to engage with what we do not know, and this but enflames and exacerbates our sense of being helpless. But at the heart of this kind of prayer we remain powerless.

To choose to wait in the 'black dark' and to invite the unknown to move towards us and into us is not only to identify with others, it is also to face the enemy who comes at us, who is against peace and justice, and is personified in greed, in lust for power, in avarice – all those forces that cannot ever wait, and which act only to make a killing.

"For it is not against human enemies that we have to struggle, but against the sovereignties and the powers who originate the darkness in this world, the spiritual army of evil in the heavens." (Ephesians 6.12)

So why choose to do it? Simply because it is what Christ chooses to do. It is the hanging there, helplessly fixed to a cross and letting it all come at you. It is Black Friday before it is Good Friday. It is the Three Hours.

It is to put ourselves utterly at the mercy of the blank promise offered to everyone by God. Beyond those seemingly endless waves of waiting there is the Creation which is Good, *is* Good. That is the promise: beauty, love beyond imagination always coming towards us, always, for ever.

"Glory be to him whose power, working in us, can do infinitely more than we can ask or imagine." (Ephesians 3.20)

So I am wondering if there is a place for a Community of the Three Hours in the life of the prayer in which Christians engage. Hence this invitation to make a gesture with the prayer of contemplation in the world of action.

LETTER TWO
Pentecost 1987

I have wanted to write for some time and share some of the strong and varied responses to my original letter. Many people have taken such pains to think and reply. The letter seems to have been a trigger. Thank you for being so encouraging. Yes, that feels important: to encourage one another on the negative way!

But I have been asking, What shall I write now, and how?

The spur came in the news a few days ago. The voice said, "World Development...the population is increasing by one million every five days, one hundred and fifty new lives every minute...Perhaps it can be stopped only by a plague (Aids?), or natural disaster or nuclear accident or war."

The Four Horsemen ride. What is the use? What sort of God is this that the trials get harder and the path gets steeper? Are we to get the world's ecology right – only so that more people can survive? Are we to redistribute the world's wealth – only so that more people can survive? Are we to improve the world's health –

only so that more people can survive? Why not let them continue to kill one another in Northern Ireland? It can seem a small price to pay.

And what of our own puny sufferings? Well, they seem like a pinprick, a million times invisible to the naked eye.

I need to pause, and ponder an amazing thing. The staggering mystery is that in the heart of this teeming, pouring-out universe, where we seem virtually less than nothing, we are in fact unique and infinitely valuable. Can I believe this? Dare I believe this?

So...move into the vastness, the void: inhabit it, love it. Give your best attention to detail. Don't skimp on affection and time for persons. Slow down: resist the pressure to go faster and faster. Listen more. Talk less. Abandon words. Move into the mystery. Leave the known for the unknown. Be an equal to those to whom you listen, not a superior. Reduce, slim, shed. The more wealth you let go of the more you have. Without becoming impoverished, live simply, be poor. Be prodigally generous. Be unrelentingly merciful. These are all stations on the same line. The only real disaster, says Roger, Prior of Taizé, is loss of love.

I find it hard, this block of time, this three hours. As someone said, "Sure, I will wholeheartedly give my life for the peace of the world. The only trouble is that I keep taking it back the very next day." Often I want to avoid it; yet the whole of Friday revolves around it. It is a hollow place, and sometimes I have to con myself into keeping the time by linking it to some event, some accident, some key meeting on the international stage. I am being asked to drop everything and go to the disaster area, the hospital, the conference.

Sometimes, though, I am glad the time is simply there. It then seems to offer a proper focus, a still centre for a world knocked senseless.

Someone asked if I was being too hard on myself and on others. Maybe. Yet there is almost a compulsion, a dark desire, an energy. After all, it seems such a little thing to give.

Also this: moment by moment, I can still choose to carry on or to stop. And that is in contrast to those who have no choice, those with whom I seek to share these few minutes of life each week. At the end of the three hours I can move into something else, move away quickly and make a cup of tea.

It is an attempt to share Christ's pain, no matter how hit and miss it feels. The little book of readings from Julian of Norwich, *Enfolded in Love*, published by Darton, Longman, and Todd, has this extract which puts it well for me.

> This showing of Christ's pain filled me full of pain…Then I thought, I little knew what pain it was I asked for, and like a fool regretted it, thinking that if I had known what it would be like, I should not have prayed to suffer it. For I thought this pain was worse than death itself, my pain. I thought, Is any pain like this? And I was answered in my mind: Hell is a different pain, for then there is despair. But of all pains that lead to salvation, this is the worst pain – to see your love suffer.

I don't always do it all, though I intend to. A late start usually fouls it up. And I do suspend it if another's need seems paramount.

The best I can do for now is to attach some remarks from letters I have received.

* Thank you. Don't put me on any list, don't organize me. I agree with you. I am detaching myself from many good associations. The space has to be found somehow.

* I am sure I would invent work in order to defer this closest encounter with Christ.

* There can't be many people with the time to 'face the nothing' every Friday.

* I am so bad at the prayer bit.

* The void is very positive if we do not automatically fight it.

* The gap between God and humanity is full of power.

* Intercession is being willing to allow the things prayed for to happen within you.

* It is not a choice between 'active' and 'passive': the one flows into the other.

* Yes! I'll do my bit, but what does it actually mean?

* I very much need to go into the riches of a prayer life and find it hard because the commitment to justice is so often lacking in people.

* When I was in labour I was a coward. I kept feeling that if only I had a few minutes to build up my courage I would be able to cope. But labour didn't wait for me. I feel now that I want to be given time to grow, to change before I say Yes, and there is nothing else to say except Yes.

Here are a couple of quotations from Thomas Merton that may be helpful. They were sent by another of those who have written.

Let me seek then the gift of silence, and poverty, and solitude, where everything I touch is turned into prayer, where the sky is my prayer, the birds are my prayer, the wind in the trees is prayer, for God is all in all.

I want to add, For the brickwork through the window is my prayer, this closed door is my prayer, this traffic crawl is my prayer, such is the penetrating beauty of silence. (Rest in peace, Thomas Merton.)

Many are avidly seeking but they alone find who remain in continual silence...Every man who delights in a multitude of words, even though he says admirable things, is empty within. If you love truth, be a lover of silence. Silence, like the sunlight, will illuminate you in God and will deliver you from the phantom of ignorance. Silence will unite you to God himself...

LETTER THREE
All Saintstide *1987*

I feel the need more and more to stand up and shout, "Stop!"

I seem to hear more and more voices around, ordinary voices inside and outside the Church crying out, "Tell me how to stop."

I seem to hear more and more about people who are being drawn to the stopping place, to silence, to the intersection where you have to stop in order to discover which way to go. It's as if they are saying, "When I get to the intersection, how do I put the brakes on so that I don't go past?"

The daily careering around seems to have become pre-determined, preset, and we have become demon drivers. How do you stop the vehicle of daily action which seems to drive on and on and steamrollers all sensitivity and originality, all decent imagination and feelings of self-worth, flattening utterly any sound which may resemble a still small voice?

There is the 'idiot' word in each of us, the 'fool's word'. It is a key word, and a source of new life. More and more people know that something is dead wrong at the core of their lives, that they are not centred, and that somehow that idiot word is the key for them – if only we can stop long enough to give ourselves a chance of hearing it. It is our own true word, a word of kindness and compassion. But we do not even stop to wonder if it might be something we need to hear. We half want to stop, we half want to go on. It is perhaps a mercy that we are at least torn between the two.

To come to silence is the clue for many, to stop and to be silent. It is half the meaning of contemplation. (The other half is to look in God's direction.)

I believe we need to be disciplined about this, so that each and every day the car that is going at breakneck speed simply *stops*. Otherwise we are in danger of plunging off the road. The choice may be to fall into the chasm of a deathly silence, or deliberately

to stop and to drop into the silence within. We need to temper all
our doing. Each and every day. We must will the breaking of this
deterministic chain of activities. Lord, give us the will to enter
into a daily silence.

I also believe that each week we need to set aside a longer time,
not only long enough to pay our dues, but also long enough to get
the fidgets, to feel it is a waste of time, perhaps to be disconcerted
because the silence is leading us down towards that hidden idiot
word which is a precious gift from a kind God.

To be serious about this really does matter. It is all too easy to
make a gesture in the right direction, but the fearful part of ourselves gets in the way of going on long enough so that we are
actually *changed*. In time we shall find that the smaller silences of
every day prepare us for the longer times. And only in due time,
as we drop further into our own inner chasms and caves deep
underground, will we notice a new and strange light beginning to
show.

Oh, these are fine words from someone nestling away there
in the back of beyond, behind the fells of western Cumbria, far
away from the insidious swirling pressures of metropolis. Maybe.
All I know is that it sometimes feels harder when you are tucked
away in the wild, and in any event I find it extraordinarily difficult to make the gesture of stopping every day – and handing the
driving over.

Yes, the beauty of the hills is all around, and that clearly helps,
but it is in the chasm of silence that sometimes I catch a glimpse
of what I can only call the *beauty* of God. The idiot word is about
this, as well as all those other lovely things, the kindness and the
compassion, and the rest. It is all about beauty and praise. And if
my life is to be anything of God for others and not merely the gift
of my ego self to others, so that they too may glimpse that divine
beauty, then I have to face that beauty myself and to receive
it gratefully – as pure gift. To face the beauty of real love is not
all easy, never comfortable. Part of me would still shelter in the
shaded valleys of half-truths and the petty rewards that come
from helping people.

Someone described the chasm of silence as the silence before creation. And yes, the silence *is* for happiness and contentment and quiet laughter. That is the gift in it. It is there to take off the brittle edge of our deeply serious and earnestly desperate face and to open our eyes again with wonder. It is to be full of thankfulness, and therefore full of hope, even in the swirling darkness of the age through which we live.

Do you know the diary of a young Jewish woman which she kept from 1941 to 1943, *Etty*? Her gratitude to God grew bigger and lighter the nearer the Holocaust closed in. At the extermination camp, as she waited, she said:

> I thank You for helping me to bear everything and for letting so little pass me by. I know that a new and kinder day will come, and there is only one way of preparing the new age, and that is to live it even now in our hearts. Somewhere inside me I feel so light, without the least bitterness and so full of strength and love. I would so much like to help prepare the new age.

Our prayer of silence in the dark chasm is the carrier of that promise.

We have to be willing to release our ego surface selves into the darkness, a release which takes us beyond the surfeit of daily troubles and opportunities. It is as if an invitation from God is sounding ever more clearly, "Who will go down for me?" I think there are many who recognize this, however hard it is for them to respond.

All the great writers and contemplative people in Christian history say that when you go deep into the silence and solitude of the chasm, yes, you are indeed alone. Yet, paradoxically, you become more intimate with all the peoples of the world, not less: you are not shut off at all. You become more empty so that there is more space in you to be filled. Usually we are so evasive that we fill up our lives with the people and notions we want to be of service to – and those we want to be of service to us – and we screen off those whom we do not want. But in becoming ever more silent we discover that this screening process fades. The whole world comes towards us, enters us. And surprise, surprise, we can be greatly encouraged by the sense of solidarity this gives, in both suffering and joy, with all those who arrive at our house now that we have room for them.

At the heart of you, you are not a blasted heath, windswept, withered with the bitterness of being alone and unlovable, but a meeting place like a good inn where humanity gathers and brings its warmth. And in this way we show something of the glory of God.

The unknown author of *The Cloud of Unknowing* wrote this: "All men living in earth be wonderfully holpen of this work, thou wottest not how." We do not know how it happens, but it does.

And this from Alan Ecclestone: "What do you do in an age when God keeps silent? You go down, and wait, and watch your picture of God changing, always ready at a moment's notice to move into a larger room."

All this is by way of encouraging you to persevere in pursuing silence, in practising contemplation, where you fix your gaze only on God, allowing all else to fall away. "Lift up thine heart unto God with a meek stirring of love; and mean Himself and none of His goods." (*The Cloud of Unknowing*)

It is "a swink and a sweat" having to look silently and often darkly into your own face as you seek for God, but perhaps with this sense of solidarity as we move more into silence and solitude, what we are being called to is to participate in a massive refusal of the spirit of the present age, with its tunnel vision of where everything has to fit and be accounted for, to be cost-effective, to be able to be grasped and controlled, to be useful, where achievements, marked and graded, become a god. It is a giant equation where in the end zero equals zero.

As we become a 'resistance movement' against these pressures, we are not to expect anything neat and tidy. We are being prepared to be led in unknown directions, to be one of God's loose ends, where nothing is certain and we have to learn to trust our own deepest intuitions and to be guided from within. We have to allow ourselves to be penetrated by the total mercy of all things and to rely on that mercy for our strength.

If it feels as if you have been belaboured by the word 'silence', and are left feeling heavy, this is only a measure of how little I have travelled along the contemplative way. The true contemplative would deal with such a weighty mystery much more lightly and jocularly. In any event I am telling you only what you already know.

"And therefore, if thou wilt stand and not fall, cease never in thine intent, but beat evermore on this cloud of unknowing that is betwixt thee and thy God with a sharp dart of longing love." (*The Cloud of Unknowing*)

LETTER FOUR
Pentecost 1988

There is a story of people who kept splashing through a large pond on their journeys to and fro. Invited to look into the pool as soon as they had crossed, they could see only mud and slurry. Invited to stay and rest, and to look into the pool again after an hour, they could see clearly into its hidden depths and look at everything that was there.

That is the challenge: to look clearly, with a single focus, a laser eye. As we look, we are to recall or allow to be recalled the few basic truths that guide our lives. For there are only a few: all the rest are variations on a theme, however beautiful and unique the music we are called upon to play. Granted that God never withdraws the promises to us or the gifts, almost the only word we hear in response to our question, "How shall I sing the Lord's song in a strange land?" is this: "Come, gaze into the pool. Listen to your own music. Play it again."

For most of the people who respond to this letter, the urgency and the longing is all about coming into that single gaze and staying there. We are to dig through layer after layer until we reach the core of our being where all that is precious is held. We are to make time for that long process. And this is particularly so in the these present times which are so sleek and fat and forgetting.

> We are concerned
> with a cleansing of the heart;
> the gaze of the single heart
> is able to bear
> the single light
> divinely shining
> without any setting or motion.
> Not only is the single heart
> able to bear the light
> but it is also able to abide in it.

For most people the Three Hours is not possible, it is not their way. Yet they so often say that they are glad about it, glad it's happening, are encouraged simply by knowing that. And some can make smaller commitments around it, each in his or her unique way. Certainly it is not there to make people feel guilty, feel that they ought to be doing more of that sort of thing. If we approach it like a body building exercise towards perfection, the very practice itself will soon disillusion us. It can be but a focus for ourselves, humbly entered into, while others are able to gather somewhere within range, pleased to dwell where they can be warmed by the knowledge of its happening and of their own small contributions.

All this is by way of a simple reminder to one another, gently and gladly speaking of the way we must go. And this is a reminder of something that we already know about ourselves, once we have unsmothered all those oh-so-early scripts. You know as well as I do that to be filled with the darkness of God is crucial, but, writes Brian, "we need to be reminded and reminded lest we be entirely overcome."

The Three Hours seems to be about exploring what it means to *wait*. This does not mean that we abandon all activities. It is more an *inside* waiting. It is to recognize that waiting, the longing, patient or impatient, is itself an aspect of God's Presence. We cannot get nearer than the stillness of the waiting, for in the stillness God is there.

It is God who is waiting, and we are as much waiting in and with God as for God. The emptiness, the slow stillness, the lack of expectation, the lack of movement, the flatness of waiting without conditions: all this is as God is, now.

"Whoever has waited without words has seen the Father."

Such *inside* waiting enlarges the emptiness, and it is in that emptiness that the day of God may be revealed. Anna wrote last Advent, "Would Mary's obedience have been any less important had she miscarried? Does fruitfulness, fertility, the Kingdom have its meaning in the thing that *follows* the waiting? Or is it in the waiting itself?"

She reminds us of the story of the young disciple who had evidently broken the contemplative silence with the question, "What's next?" "There's no 'next'," says the guru. "This is it."

A further thought: can this waiting actually help to create a breathing space, an empty space for those who find themselves so often without any space at all? Frank Chikane, as general secretary of the South African Council of Churches, has written this on the debate about violence and non-violence:

> There may be times where there is a space within which the debate can take place, but there is a time when this space is so violated, when circumstances so squeeze or constrict it that it ceases to exist.

Most white people in South Africa (this was written in 1988) can masquerade as non-violent, peace-loving people because they live in an artificially created space which is maintained by violence against those outside it. The oppressed exist where their space has been eliminated.

LETTER FIVE
Advent 1988

Waiting in the prayer which is darkness is hard to do. Prolonged waiting is harder. Yet it is indispensable.

The disciples asked, "What is the hardest act a person can perform?" The master answered, "Sitting in meditation." "Wouldn't that lead to inaction?" "It is inaction." "Is action, then, inferior?" "Inaction gives life to actions. Without it they are dead." (Anthony de Mello, *One Minute Wisdom*)

This is about letting go of the destructive pictures of myself that come and go in my mind, letting go of thoughts good and bad, of feelings and desires and people. I have to allow them to vanish. Everything I know about myself is to be dismissed as it arises, so that the greater truth of my greater self may emerge, the one I don't know, who is much closer to God than the self I see.

Waiting in prayer for The Three Hours is about staying closer to a crucifixion. It is about being so limp in the waiting that we expect nothing.

T. S. Eliot, in 'East Coker', the second of his *Four Quartets*, suggested that we should wait with neither hope nor love, for that would be to hope for and love the wrong things. The hope and the love are all in the waiting. For Brother Roger of Taizé it is to hope beyond hope. And if this be a waiting in the darkness, so be it. There are many darknesses to be endured.

Bridget has written: "...loving often means waiting, a holding back, a standing still, a refraining from doing what is not mine to do, a very disciplined making of space."

At the same time many people seem to know that the waiting is also a setting free from the tyranny of these pictures of ourselves which constantly threaten to squeeze and manipulate everything in creation into some predetermined frame. For those who wait regularly in prayer there often seems to be a release, as if the waiting is a coiled spring of new energy which afterwards propels them out into life.

To try and make sense of the time of waiting, or to try and make it useful, or to ask what happens in it, is to impose too much, wanting things to happen on our terms. It doesn't work like that. What seems to occur is that something is forming in the silence that is impossible to discern at the time: all seems darkness and chaos. But out of it something clear and creative does at times emerge. We gain a new perception of ourselves, different from that which we had before we entered the silence and the darkness. And this can be a new lightness, a new joy.

It reminds me of those Sisters at Burnham Abbey. They embrace their Three Hours so eagerly and believe it to be such a privilege. There is such lightness about them. In a very different setting, that of family life, Ruth writes to tell of barricading herself in the bathroom, finding it a refuge in which to kneel, thankful for the desire to do it, and eager for the arrival of those precious moments.

It would be so much easier to stay with those pictures of myself, hanging them on my inner walls to look at. To push them away as soon as they arrive leaves me with an unavoidable con- frontation with the Other. I want to keep on dodging that. For me, there are three reminders that help me to wait and to stay there in the silence. I share them for taking or leaving.

First is another story from *One Minute Wisdom*. A disciple fell asleep and dreamed that he had entered Paradise. To his aston- ishment he found his Master and the other disciples sitting there, absorbed in meditation. "Is this the reward of Paradise?" he cried. "Why, it is exactly the sort of thing we did on earth." He heard a Voice exclaim, "Fool! You think those meditators are in Paradise? It is just the opposite. Paradise is in the meditators."

My second reminder is this. You know how it is when an old friend arrives unexpectedly at the front door and can't stay long. You are taken utterly by surprise and delighted. You want to put everything else to one side and spend as much time together as you can. This is how it can be with time set aside for waiting in prayer, and we do everything we can to dodge it as it approaches. I often find myself muttering, I can't possibly give the time today. There's too much on. Or, I'll just do this or that first. And before I know it the time is eaten into and gone. The excuses follow. "You know how it is, Lord, you see the demands on my time."

So I remind myself that the time of prayer is like that old friend who knocks inconveniently at my door, and I joyfully set aside everything else and spend time with this most precious arrival.

And my third reminder. I use a very simple mantra, a few words at most, repeating them again and again and again. ('Mantra' means 'cleansing of the mind'.) I hold on to it for dear life and use it to hit on the head everything that comes up during the prayer of waiting. It is like sounding a great gong inside, boom after boom. It is as if I am driving at speed along a motorway, tempted by distractions and sideshows but determined to keep my eyes fixed on the road ahead, all my wits tuned to the track.

I find this is a clean discipline. It lops off distractions, cleans up my scattered mind, deals healthily with those pictures of myself, stops me playing around, cutting down self-indulgence and the desire to rest yet again. It helps me to stay put. This is 70 mph stuff.

I need to leave my ego behind so that my new self can emerge. The real person, whom I do not and cannot yet recognize, who is deep in the heart of God, is ahead.

The Cloud of Unknowing (chapter 7) sets the precedent.

> If you want to pierce the cloud of unknowing between yourself and God, and if you feel by grace that you are called by God...take but a little word...and fasten this word to your heart...This word will be your shield and spear...With this word you shall beat upon this cloud and this darkness and smite down all manner of thought.

The one word of my mantra simplifies me, assists me to focus. But to say that it is 'simple' is not to say that it is 'easy'. John Main is a contemporary teacher of stillness and silence by way of a Christian mantra. His description of distractions is superb. "The mind is a mighty tree filled with monkeys."

LETTER SIX
Pentecost 1989

Whatever else this Community of the Three Hours is about, at its heart is a staying still in silent prayer so that the peace and justice of God may be more clearly seen in the world, and associating this prayer in some way with the Good Friday Three Hours of prayer at the Cross. To want to wait in silence, for however long or short a time, is a gift. We have been given it to use and practise.

Last Christmas I received a letter from a community of Lutheran Sisters in Hamburg, the Ordo Pacis. One sentence has stayed with me these past months, more so than anything else that I have read. "It requires strong faith to endure the nearness of the risen Lord, embraced by his glance but not seeing, not grasping, but empty, and yet still believing."

I find that so often I have turned away. I usually call this 'distractions', and it is a familiar theme to all who have stumbled along this path. But more deeply perhaps, I turn away because I cannot bear to look long in a particular direction, into the darkness where the Lord is. I cannot bear too much reality. It is too much. It is immense. I have a longing to look towards Jesus, towards the Presence, yet the brilliance of looking towards and yet *not* seeing, that is too much. I look into a darkness, into an emptiness, yet I have the intuition that in that dark, in that nothing, 'It', 'The truth', is all there, waiting to be found and seen. It is a dazzling perception, immense. I wait, expecting nothing, demanding nothing, yet in faith.

In silent prayer we are asked to plunge into that darkness and quench everything we know, every feeling, every thought, so that we become empty. That is what is *required*. Nor am I to give value to anything that might happen, for that is far less than the presence of God, a presence that is indeed *immense*. And because it is all too much, I allow whatever is within me to turn me aside and comfort me with the usual distractions and the pictures of reality that I can manage. Note that: *I* can manage. For here is something that I know, rather than something I do not know, that something that is a mystery.

Yet for my encouragement I seem to meet more and more people who in a straightforward, matter-of-fact way know that in the darkness and the waiting there is presence and not absence. There is a nearness, sometimes almost palpable, often not. But they simply get on with it. They are willing to stand, within a firm discipline, redressing the balance between doing and being, so that being in the silence *in* God becomes least as important as doing things *for* God. They are seeking to discover God within their own immense depths, and they are not looking away towards an object of worship. And it *is* a risk...

Recently I was in a cave in complete darkness. After a while lights were switched on and we saw the most beautiful stalagmites and stalactites. It was ravishing, a joy to behold. Then the lights were put out. We knew the beauty was there but we couldn't see it any more, couldn't even remember it. In some of Shakespeare's plays there are stage directions about 'dark lanterns'. The presence of the risen Lord is a dark lantern.

I spent a Quiet Day with Alan Ecclestone recently. Here are a few of the things he said.

He reminded us that the silence is the promise of God's presence. The Word is forming in us, through us, for us.

He pointed to Jesus's unwavering trust in the silence he calls Father. He hears in silence and the Father replies in silence.

And this. If, deep in the silence, we allow the Word to take shape in us, we are participating in the reconstruction of the world. Because we are not silent enough, the world is not silent enough, and we are missing half of its cues. We have to nerve ourselves to help the world to grow in its memory of God by holding ourselves to God. We have to hold everything that we already know to God, so that what we do not know about God may emerge.

In the babel, so much has to be unlearned, undone, if new growth is to occur. And silence can help us do this. But we must also lay aside the desire for results, things we can measure. It is no use placing the silence against a clipboard, against a balance-sheet, trying to estimate a spiritual budget. Put this in, get this out: a smart accounting system to assess the state of the nation's – or of our own – soul. We are so smart. Surely we can do it...

We need to put some markers down in our daily lives that can help us discount this kind of material evaluation. In a complicated world, with its tangles of evil, such markers need to be few and simple, or we can get enmeshed in bewilderment and find our-selves distracted yet again. But let the markers do something to set us free, something that is contradictory to the world of calculation.

Here are four of mine, in no particular order: choosing to practise hospitality, whether convenient or inconvenient; choos-ing to be generous, with the feeling of going too far, of being extravagant; choosing to be satisfied with less, enjoying shedding, and so creating space, satisfied with the lowly, refusing to acquire; choosing a discipline of time simply to be aware with God. This last may involve renouncing something, but to be besieged with busyness crushes sensitivity and defeats the work of creation. (And we also need what Francis Dewar calls 'loitering' time.)

I finish with a poem by Catherine Hewitt, 'Disillusionment':

> Love begins with disillusionment.
> How can an image be sustained for ever,
> A God, a friend, a child, a lover?
> We only love the clothes we have imposed
> On the mystery in which we are enclosed.
> When stifled Reality struggles to be free
> We are appalled at the strange face we see,
> Call it ugly, base, deceitful; feel betrayed.

Truth seems an enemy, which tears aside
The fabricated world in which we hide.
And only when I myself can bear
To look at what I really am, will I perceive
That I too am a fabrication of dreams,
Born of fear, which projected on to all that is
Images to shelter me from life's moving stream.
So that the truth which looked out of my illusions
Was a threat, which shook to its foundations
The insecure world of my imagination.
Let the world fall apart. Look with wonder
At what is, laid bare. Start the adventure
Of living. Emerge from your self-made fantasy
Of life as you feel it ought to be.
Dare to see
And be free.

LETTER SEVEN
All Saintstide 1989

I read recently a series of articles devoted to old age. It was full of landmarks for the journey of spiritual growth, a growth which may be more a descent than an ascent. Go lower, says the voice, go lower if you would walk more closely with God, you in me and I in you. The articles showed how important it is to enter the prayer of silent waiting, no matter what age we are.

Those who are old feel themselves to be increasingly power-less, useless, helpless, and frail compared with how they used to see themselves. By necessity they spend a lot more time hanging around, waiting. Lives seem empty that were once full and fulfilled. There seems to be so much loss.

We don't of course have to be old to know something of this.

And the challenge is to accept in as loving a way as we are able whatever comes along, simply as it is happening. We can begin to learn that such times are treasures hidden in this requirement from God to let go more deeply into the darkness of being helpless.

It was Robert Browning who wrote:

> Grow old along with me,
> The best is yet to be,
> The last of life for which the first was made.

Commenting on this, Stephen Verney writes, "Perhaps it is through the powerlessness of old people that God is praying his own prayer." And he quotes a Russian mystic approaching her own death, "There are so many more of us old people these days, I think God is creating for himself a pool of obedience."

This confirms for me the importance of beginning to practise this silent waiting while we can still fend for ourselves. We know that underneath our vigour and bright action and commitments and purposeful living there are already intimations of frailty and uselessness. Our best endeavours are so fragile, so fleeting. And we often escape into activity to avoid this reality.

We are called to turn and embrace these feelings, to rest with them as a proper part of our lives, to make ourselves at home with them. We need to let these images rise into awareness, to acknowledge them and to let them go. We are to give them room in our lives, practising being helpless now rather than wait until we are forced to do so. For then it will be all the more painful and difficult. It is the emptiness of accepting the loss of all things, so that we may be the more ready to embrace our dependence on God.

It is a kind of death to relinquish those precious pictures we guard of ourselves, that, sometimes without knowing it, we hang on to so fiercely. It is not that in themselves they are bad: there is a place for affirming ourselves, made as we are in the good image of God. But if we only affirm, our image grows and becomes inflated and we do not recognize how false and transient it is. We need also to see them in proportion and to practise letting them go, moving through them beyond them, emptying ourselves of them. Then when they appear again in our active lives we shall be able to see them as the fraction of the truth about us that they really are. They have value, they have power, but given too much, they are dangerous. There is much more in us, and the gateway to that more is the helplessness and the emptying.

The search for truth always takes us into spaces that are empty of all that is familiar. But enter them in silence, in waiting, in darkness, and we may know a peace and a reality not known before. See yourself now through the eyes of old age.

And the younger you are the better. St John of the Cross was only forty-nine when he died, yet his 'waiting' has resonated for human beings ever since. I long for such a youthful passion in all of us, an embracing, paradoxically, of the letting go, of the emptiness.

The more we accept how little our actions are, how frail, how empty, however significant they are in the outer world, even making history, the more space we allow ourselves, the less the great ME occupies, the more we can welcome others in, welcome the creation of becoming ever more compassionate as we are filled with the other and dedicated to the other. In what begins as a seemingly totally dark, negative lack, there enters a fullness, a love and a strength made perfect in weakness.

Silent prayer, slowly but surely, through all the stages of a lifetime, takes away, gently but firmly, all our illusions. The less we live with them, the more we live with God, and the more totally we become compassionate. This is the goal of life for all who thirst for God.

Here is a story from Anthony de Mello's *Song of the Bird*:

A lover knocks at the door of his beloved. "Who knocks?" asks the beloved from within. "It's me," says the lover. "Then go away. The house will not hold both you and me." The rejected lover goes away into the desert, meditating for months on end, pondering the words of the beloved. Finally he returns and knocks at the door again. "Who knocks?" "It is you." The door immediately opens.

LETTER EIGHT
Pentecost 1990

Some people get alarmed and upset when I talk about going into the darkness. "There he goes again, old doom and gloom. What's the matter with him? Where's the joy in this man's faith?"

The Community of the Three Hours precisely does choose to go into the darkness. As well as that darkness over the whole earth from the sixth to the ninth hour on the day Jesus died on the cross, there is a vast darkness out there – and in here – and if evangelism is about anything it must include that going into it.

To pray *into* the silence is to pray *into* the darkness. To be still and silent as an act of prayer is a crucifixion of mind and language. The notice in the front of your personal shop window is 'Everything has to go!' You are having a closing-down sale in order to move into new premises. And for prayer that is more a process than a single event. To be faithful is to be continually changing premises.

Our thoughts and our words seem to be helpful in our desire to get hold of the truth, but they are only sliproads on to the motorway of the prayer which leads us more deeply, in the silence, into the reality that is indeed the truth.

Of course we prefer the noise of our actual motorways to stopping and becoming still and silent. The very prospect fills most people with dread. It seems to us at first that to sit back and do nothing is to be lazy, but to be still, and to offer that stillness, requires more energy than it does to run. It is not that we ourselves are being energetic, being powerful, but that energy, power, is being drawn out of us.

This is to try and put into words something profound that is happening well below the surface of our being, at the very source of our energy. When we are still, the world comes and takes, down there in the darkness, from the source of our being. Is it the difference between the stillness of the battery and the light shining from the the torch?

An exhausted woodcutter wasted time and energy chopping wood with a blunt axe because he didn't have time to stop and sharpen the blade. To become still in the darkness is to sharpen prayer's blade.

Then the work can be done, the work of intercession, which is to allow what is being prayed for to happen within us. We are taken into what is fraught and difficult for others, ourselves feeling more and more powerless, without quite knowing what is happening, except that energy is being drawn from us. Afterwards we may be quite worn out.

To choose the prayer of darkness is to choose that process. I have no wish to claim this as the best way of praying. But it is a gift in its own right, and if it has been given to us we have to honour it. All the energy is poured out from Jesus in the darkness of those three hours. It takes him into his death. It reveals more and more of the truth of who he is.

We experience it as a loss, for it takes us away from our 'worldly' self and closer to other human beings. The deeper we go the nearer we come to others, in the place where we are like them, and they are like us. Stripped of our individual dressage, of all that marks us out as different from others, superior or inferior, we are remarkably alike in our nakedness. The more we strive to be different, the further we separate ourselves from our neighbour. It is strange that it takes becoming naked in the dark to find out what true communion with others is all about. Our new identity comes from what we have in common with others rather than from what makes us different.

The psalmist speaks of our entering a large room of freedom. But we have to enter it via the darkness, this empty chamber at the root of our being where our universal nature dwells with the one creative Word, where we become as one with that Word. It is the place where "deep calls to deep", as Psalm 42 puts it. Meister Eckhart points out that the more we allow the silence to sound, to reverberate, within us, the more we experience joy and sorrow, not separately in a sequence of time, but simultaneously. It is like standing in a large dark cave with a splendid echo. You hear the second word coming back to you long before the sound of the first has died away. You hear yourself speaking twice, but sounding the two notes at the same time.

I remember a woman who stood up in the middle of a conference with tears pouring down her face and calling out, "How is it possible to experience such joy and sorrow at the same time?"

For Eckhart, to be in movement is also to be in total repose. That is echoed by modern physics which speaks of waves and particles, depending on how you look. What at first seems as if it is only darkness, or only light, may be known together, as if a torch were flashing on and off at such a frequency that we are no longer aware of the difference.

If we can learn to trust ourselves to the darkness, what is at first a kind of death begins to be experienced as new life. An ending becomes a beginning. Innocence is restored. It is more than a wistful gazing at a Christmas crib, for a moment or two longing for a different world, but even that can encourage us to journey into the darkness in search of that light.

A PS via Eckhart about distractions in dark prayer. We are to imagine ourselves looking at all the different images and emotions that flicker disconcertingly on and off the screen of the mind, and to realize that they are not ME. I AM is looking at them. They are separate from the self that truly is, from I AM. It is not so much a matter of "Father, hear the prayer I offer" as "Father, hear the prayer I AM."

It is good to be in the company of such fellow travellers.

LETTER NINE
All Saintstide to Advent 1990

I am indebted to those who have said to me, "Write on," and to those who have said, "I don't understand all of what you write, but keep writing it." And occasionally those who remark, "Have you read such-and-such? It's the same territory."

One or two reminders seem appropriate. When people say that contemplative silence is not for them, rather the way of action, I need to say that to be still in silent prayer is an action, an intervention of a very direct kind into the order of things. It is not doing nothing. Christ in Gethsemane is not doing nothing. The doing is in the waiting. For the same reason, deliberately to make time for silence is not artificial or unnatural, but it *is* discipline. Discipline is an action. It is we who are artificial, out of line with our true selves if we cannot be still when required to be, either for ourselves or for others. Think of the stillness of the wildlife photographer, waiting, waiting, for the one right moment.

Each time we enter silent prayer it is a choice of suffering. To remain in silent prayer is to choose the immense struggle between bare, ferocious, unrelenting Ego and the presence of God, a struggle which goes on in the heart of me and so in the heart of the universe. Each time of silent prayer, as Robert describes clearly and directly, is 'a little Gethsemane': Gethsemane, the place of dark waiting.

And 'dark prayer' is simply 'praying into the darkness'. It is nothing special or rare, and it is not only for the few. It is a place most, if not all of us, have to arrive at, to recognize it, and to wait there. We know we are entering it when words give out, when feelings vanish. It is the time when we are faced with unknowing. There are no signs. We have to stay with nothing, to know an absence, a blankness. We are to be lost, to be empty.

The disciple said, "I have come to you with nothing in my hands." The master replied, "Drop it at once."

Dark prayer is the darkness of the 'underearth' where things grow without being seen. To allow God's word and purpose to grow in us, through us, pouring out through us into the rest of creation, without being seen by us, or by anybody: that is the task. We are black-dark to what is happening. There is no light: yet we trust God's promises.

Simply to be there in the dark of utter unknowing: that is Gethsemane. And Golgotha is prayer at its most dark.

Dark prayer is one of God's ways of penetrating the vast dark that is the mystery at the heart of the world. God is using us to stand in the dark. It is a gift to us of 'standing-in', in order to bring more of the mystery into the light. The creation of goodness begins in darkness. We descend into the mystery, called by love to be makers with God at that formless place where chaos and terror are confronted and resolved and something new is created.

It all sounds very grand. Such big words frighten us, and we can easily find ourselves saying, Not for me. Yet I am trying to write of something that is so very simple, something that is already *there* in the depths of us. It is an ordinary, if not easy, daily task, a making of the Kingdom of God in hidden and obscure ways.

As we mature on this inner journey, as we trust the process of taking risks, we find that the darkness is not without peace, and it becomes at times a steady resting place where we do not sleep but become more alert. Occasionally it turns to awe and wonder. If we persevere peacefully, accepting the dark unknowing as a gift, we touch the outer edges of glory.

We may then become alert to its happening in the outer world. For so much is changing within and without. It is as if we are in the midst of an immense unveiling (that is another word for 'apocalypse'). Humankind is being lowered through layer after layer of new understanding and challenge, down into the 'ancient unknown', becoming aware of new powers of being, new possibilities of communion.

For example, this time last year we were celebrating freedom with whole symphonies being sung on the Berlin Wall, aware of people all over eastern Europe breaking into the daylight out of the darkness. Rocks split, graves were broken open, and veil after veil fell from human eyes. Idols collapsed into a heap of dust. At the same time, new chasms of darkness were opening, as the energy held down for so long began to be expressed. What would happen to these pulses of frustration and these tremblings of hope? As we begin to meet new neighbours, what new language of communion will have to be written?

How much darkness can we tolerate? How deep do we have to go? How can the centre hold? Well, it cannot unless there are watchers in the darkness, living in their silent suffering and dark adoration the watchfulness of Christ, breaking down in the roots of their own being the hostility between known and unknown.

'Dark adoration' may seem a strange phrase. What is it about, this standing there in dark adoration? It is to become aware of a desire beyond desire, of a hope beyond hope. It is a riddle yet it is as clear as the day. It is a gift that brings both peace and pain. We are in the midst of God, for whom dark and light are both alike, and we are incessantly called by that name.

It is as if God is saying, "You won't really know what you are doing standing there. I only just know about it myself." In the end there is always laughter.

Anthony de Mello, in his first volume entitled *Prayer of the Frog*, tells this story.

> The master was in an expansive mood. So his disciples sought to learn from him the stages he had passed through in his search for the divine. "God first led me by the hand," he said, "into the Land of Action, and there I dwelt for several years. Then he returned and led me to the Land of Sorrows, and there I lived until my heart was purged of every inordinate attachment. That is when I found myself in the Land of Love whose burning flames consumed whatever was left in me of self. This brought me to the Land of Silence where the mysteries of life and death were bared before my wondering eyes." "Was that the final stage of your quest?" they asked. "No," the master said. "One day God said,

'Today I shall take you to the innermost sanctuary of the temple, to the heart of God himself.' And I was led to the Land of Laughter."

R. S. Thomas puts it modestly enough:

> I think that maybe
> I will be a little surer
> of being a little nearer.
> That's all. Eternity
> is in the understanding
> that that little is more than
> enough.

LETTER TEN
Pentecost 1991

I find in myself a lot of fine talk about poverty of the spirit, living in poverty, living more simply that others may simply live, etc., etc. At the same time I can't fail to be aware of the richness and diversity of my existence and experience. I long for poverty and I am so far from it. Am I deluding myself? What do I do about my fine home, my fine car, the fine food I eat, the fine money I have to spend, my fine friends, my fine freedom of opportunity and movement? And I seem to accumulate more and more riches in a varied and purposeful life.

God may indeed be an endless journey, as a card put it that was sent to us by the Sisters of Burnham Abbey. But we are so easily distracted on the journey, endlessly so. There is so much going on, so much to choose to do, many exciting wines to sip and sweetmeats to taste, new adventures on every page. And we run the risk of being violently and endlessly distracted by the enormous events of sadness or joy in the world.

What can it mean to have all things stripped away from us, as Jesus was stripped?

Dare I claim, with all the riches I have, that the door to poverty is silent prayer? Well, it can feel like that: the silence takes everything away, leaving me with nothing. I become poor, naked, empty. I discover that this journey that is God has nothing to do with trying new things or taking on new tasks. It is to do with going through the eye of the needle: it requires focus, an exact focus and absolute attention, with an unwavering gaze on the one thing. It is to pierce through the vast array of stimuli, good or bad, with which even the best of us are surrounded but which eventually leave us fatigued, "distracted by distraction from distraction", as Eliot put it. To be torn this way and that is to waste our energy and become exhausted. Remember that ancient teaching from the desert: Stay in your cell and it will teach you all you need to know. Silent prayer requires us to be still enough not to be knocked off centre by the bombardment of daily news and events.

The story is told of the novice who insisted that the master archer be put to the test. So the master was blindfolded and let into the great hall where all the windows were blacked out, and he was asked to shoot at the target at the far end. He waited, utterly still, balanced, in the darkness. Then he placed an arrow with gentle care and drew his bow. The arrow sped.

The novice shone his light and saw that the arrow had pierced the very centre of the target. He went up to the master, turned him round and round, and said, "Shoot again." Again there was a stillness and a waiting. Gently the master drew on his full strength and power and the arrow sped out into the darkness. When they uncovered the windows they discovered that the second arrow had split the first one in two.

The story says something about the poverty and beauty to which we are called in this way of prayer, the simple, silent prayer of virtually no words. We drop lower and lower, deeper into the cave of our hearts, allowing the arrow to move in that direction and pierce the target in the depths, in its very centre. And all the while we simply remain in the darkness. We pass through all the dazzling torments that have distracted us and wounded us, all the moments of success and of failure, and of the world saving us and failing us.

It is such a little thing, this minute contribution of our constant aiming, again and again not even hitting the target, let alone its centre. But it is to be poor. And it may also be cosmic in its significance. That sounds pretentious. But we are laying aside the clothes of our possessions and our words and our beliefs even, so that we become naked in our poverty, seeking to do this day by day as a deliberate act. But to be nearer our own true heart is also to be nearer the heart of the world, and so the movement is cosmic in scope.

It may *seem* in silent prayer that there is everything of ourselves and nothing very much of God, including all those things I am trying to let go of. Can I really believe that God is in the midst – of me? I may hold on to a few, bare, key words, and trust that their shape and their texture are shaping me – and in time I even have to let go of these.

It is as if I am being bent into the shape of the bow in the darkness, while I continue to place all my strength at the exact point from which the arrow must fly and focusing all my attention on the target. Occasionally, unpredictably, unexpectedly, there comes a moment – without seeing – when we are overwhelmed by the simplicity and the beauty of the arrow piercing the centre of the target.

Putting together some words of Max Warren, Dag Hammarsjøld, W. H. Auden, and David Jones, Jim Cotter has written (later published in *Waymarks*):

> You have to be a pioneer, journeying to places the rest of the world ignores…It is a narrow way, but do not complain – the way chose you, and you must be thankful…It is a difficult choice, but to choose what is difficult as if it were easy, that is faith…Do not retreat from the unfamiliar, nor condemn it. When a civilization turns, God may not be found at the old landmarks.

If you feel that the darkness has descended upon you as you journey on and in, maybe the darkness has chosen you.

Here is a short poem by an anonymous writer called 'Transfiguration':

This must be
the white fire they talk of
that blacks the hollows of the eyes,
makes all the looking useless.

Yet I must look.

No wonder
that I cannot see
where I am or what I am,
and all things once held dear have gone,
if I am
in the middle of it then.

I who thought I was so far off
am perhaps after all
so near?

LETTER ELEVEN
All Saintstide to Advent 1991

It is All Saints' Day, and once again Jew and Arab face each other across a conference table. People bound by ancient mutual hatred begin once again to try and ease the pain, breath by breath. Finger joints set in a claw of mistrust have to be opened ever so gently lest they only tighten. And so with Serb and Croat, Irish and Irish, black and white, and wherever else it seems that hatred almost steams out from cracks in the earth.

To stand with awareness and gentleness is the work of this dark prayer. Gentleness is a word and a reality almost lost in these intractable conflicts, yet such gentleness is the power of this dark prayer. It drains away more energy than we realize to stand thus, not least because our own harshness and impatience keeps on tearing us away from gentleness. It seems impossible to stand even for a moment, let alone stay in a place that we are tempted to think of as nothing but ultimate foolishness. To wait and to watch: as so often we feel useless.

During those three hours, there is nothing of gentleness near Jesus as he suffers and dies. Can we manage even three minutes of standing there, being there, obeying the invitation to stay with him in that darkest of places? Again, it seems impossible.

Yet the desire again and again rises up and speaks from the depths of our being, hearing the voice of the One in the darkness simply asking for companions. "I want you to be with me where I am." In the end we discover that there is nowhere else to go, nowhere better to be. To be invited into the darkness of silent prayer is an act of friendship, however startling that is when we first realize it. "Come lower," says God, "I trust you."

Little by little, we become aware of so much movement, so many cries, coming from the depths of the darkness, coming at us from all directions. We learn to receive a scraping sound, a gasp, a stifled groan, a small ecstasy, one by one as we are able. Nothing in the end is unheard, and nothing is lost, not even a hair of anyone's head. No pain is ignored: no syllable is overlooked. Everything is recognized, each with its own place.

In the deep calling to the deep below the roar of the waters, when all torrents and waves have swept over us, as they did the Psalmist (Psalm 42–43), God's word comes forth, and nothing can stop it. Our lives belly forth, we know not how. At times it feels almost like the African woman who squats on her haunches in the open desert, delivers her baby on her own, and goes on her way, leaving her child behind, for there is nothing else that she can do.

This dark prayer is so simple, so poor, so still, with hardly a word, hardly a breath. And it feels worthless, useless. And yet it

can console, not least when the emptiness is shared in the company of others. And from its heart goes forth that word, which is
one of justice. From no other place than the pain can grow the
peace where the destitute are gathered, the brutalized, the discarded, those who are passed by, who stand still while the cars
of the wealthy roar mindlessly and endlessly by. They can do no
other than wait. They have nothing unless it is given to them.
Told to stay put or told to move on, they don't matter, they have
no say in the decisions.

To be aware of them with us in the darkness challenges our
prayer at the deepest level. For they generate hatred in us. They
face us with our false gods, and it is not easy to realize that we
need their help to discard the idols. We know one another only at
such costly depths. There is no other way to freedom.

I am reminded again of my dear friend Etty, scribbling her
notes from a concentration camp where with so many of her
fellow Jews she went to her death. "No words or images are
adequate to describe nights like these…If I were to say that I
was in hell that night, what would I really be telling you?" She
sits on a bed holding a young girl who is rigid with fear, she
stands with those whose children are about to be born into the
nightmare, or with those who are alive but very sickly, she moves
among the sweat and the hysteria, with nothing but her willingness to share it with them. The only help she brings is her
helpless self.

"And yet," she says,

> late at night when the day has slunk away into the depths
> behind me, I often walk with a spring in my step along the
> barbed wire, and then time and again it soars straight from my
> heart – I can't help it, that's just the way it is, like some ele-
> mental force – the feeling that life is glorious and magnificent,
> and one day we shall be building a whole new world. Against
> every outrage and every fresh horror we shall put up one more
> piece of love and goodness…

Then, with great daring, she says,

Most people here are much worse off than they need be because they write off their longing for friends and family as so many losses in their lives, when they should count the fact that their heart is able to long so hard and to love so much among their greatest blessings.

That is also experienced by those who are exploring the gift of this dark prayer and seeking to persevere in it. Sometimes there is a spring in their heart, a quickening of the step, the sense that within all the chaos of human tumult we are indeed sharing in the making of a new world. There are not many such moments, but enough.

PS. From Matthew Fox, interpreting Meister Eckhart:

In true humility God who is truth becomes one with the truth of ourselves. There is no distance between God and us when we truly know our own depths…God does not come down to the humble person but is rather within…'The ground of the soul is dark,' says Eckhart…He urges us not be afraid of the dark, not to flee from the truth of ourselves, which is that deep down we are dark and in the dark…'To explore the darkness is the deepest kind of humility.'

LETTER TWELVE
Pentecost 1992

Returning from holiday with its long news blackout is like stepping back into the fiery furnace. I find that straightaway I am on the brink of all the world's horrors. Why do Etty Hilversum and her diaries immediately haunt my mind? Perhaps it is because we live in a world that seems like a tourist concentration camp. Every

gunshot ricochets round our living rooms. Every ravaged face,
every last breath in far-off places is reflected in the surface of our
supper trays. It is as if we wander round a flipside Disneyland,
voyeurs of the horrors and disgusted with ourselves. Our comfort
is continually discomforted.

But perhaps Etty comes to me also to rescue me. Her own
quest for prayer when she was surrounded by speechless horrors
became the more brilliant the more helpless she found herself to
be. She knew that in order to be a centre of peace in a madhouse
she had to be steeped in eternity, as if she were a firefighter who
has to be constantly drenched in water not only to stay alive but
also to be given at least the chance of saving a few people from
the fire.

> I lay in the dark with burning eyes as scene after scene of human
> suffering passed before me. I shall promise you one thing, God,
> just one very small thing: I shall never burden my today with
> cares about tomorrow. Even though this takes some practice,
> today is sufficient to itself. I shall try to help you, God, to stop my
> strength ebbing away, though I cannot vouch for it in advance.
> But one thing is becoming increasingly clear to me, that you
> cannot help us and that we must help you to help ourselves. And
> perhaps in others as well. Alas, there doesn't seem to be much you
> yourself can do about our circumstances, about our lives. Neither
> do I hold you responsible. You cannot help us, but we must help
> you and defend your dwelling place inside us to the last…I thank
> God for helping me to bear things and let so little pass by.

Lizbet writing from Edinburgh says that her life has come to
this one point: "Now I see the task of being thankful, praising,
joyful, as a task of burning through the dark. And to me, that task
springs from and is nourished by prayer." She quotes Berthold
Brecht: "There are those who dwell in darkness, there are those
who dwell in light. Those in light can be seen; those in darkness
one does not see."

And Anna Briggs in Canada comes out of a course ('History
belongs to the intercessors') to remind us through its central

theme that it is not we who pray but God who prays in us. "We *become* the breath of God, we let God breathe us into prayer." Christ already dwells in the depths of our hearts, the light already there. Prayer is the very fabric of our being if we will let it be. Helpless onlookers, robbed of action, our only recourse is to become what we already are, prayer. We are prayer from the beginning. We can descend openly into the deepest sadness and griefs which we perpetually gulp down as part of our daily diet because the resurrection is already there beneath it all.

Anna reminds us also of the poet Irina Ratushinskaya writing out of her terrible Soviet prison. "Every breath is outside the law and they cannot take that away." Every breath of prayer is beyond the laws and systems of the world, of this time and this space.

Such is our quest for prayer, itself a dark trail of helplessness. One of the most precious gifts in these times is that we keep wanting to return to prayer, to make a new beginning. This restless desire to make a new creation is a sign of eternity alive within us. To be steeped in eternity means to be willing to let go in prayer of every known thing, experience, feeling, thought, since all these are inadequate. And as we do so, God can the more fully breathe through us. Only in this way can we survive alongside those who all around us are stripped of every known thing. Otherwise we withdraw.

This silent prayer, this silent gathering of witnesses, is an acknowledgment that no matter where we start in prayer, and whatever variety of prayer we offer, in the end everything we know has gone. Only the silence remains. Faced with the presence of God and the mystery of bringing love into suffering, silence is inevitable.

So many human lives pass through our hands in the course of a day, a week, a lifetime that we must leave space within us, there must be a certain emptiness, so that as they appear, disappear, sometimes re-appear, they may somehow be refreshed by being able to rest in what may be unknown to them but known to us, *God's* presence within us and so within them.

We do not bombard them with words of prayer, we do not make verbal demands on God, that certain situations be changed. But we simply pause. We offer a breathing space. "Breathe on me breath of God, fill *them* with life anew." Perhaps they may return to their true selves, if only for a while. At the heart of their own disillusion and despair they may gain hope enough for one more day.

Our prayer, now silent, is lowered down, and we with the prayer, on a precarious dangling line of peace into the awfulness, even the scream of terror, that lies too deep, beyond tears. There, by our presence, by our prayer, there may be brought a purifying energy for endurance and change.

Our fear is that we shall fall apart, be torn apart, at that very place, that we shall not meet God or that we shall meet God and not know who it is. In the silence what are we able to recognize?

In the end there is no escape, for nothing is more certain for us human beings than the experience of suffering, not least when we are prayer, and when we seek to live the truth. Meister Eckhart says: "It is good that a person has a peaceful life; it is better that a person bear a troublesome life with patience. But best of all is that a person can have peace in the very midst of trouble."

So, to all fools, from Robert, this parable of the Fisher King:

> As a boy, the Fisher King had to spend a night in the forest before he could become king. He was visited by a fire, out of which appeared the Holy Grail, the Cup of God's Grace. A voice said, "You shall be the keeper of the Grail, that it may heal hearts." But the boy was blinded by greater visions. As he reached to take the Grail, it vanished, and his hands, left in the fire, were terribly wounded. As the boy grew, his wound deepened, until one day he had no faith left in anyone, not even in himself. He became so sick with all that he had experienced that he began to die. As he began to fade, so did his kingdom. So the people, greatly afraid, sent the king's knights to find the Grail. They roamed far and wide, but their journeys were futile.

One day, a fool wandered into the castle and found the king alone and in pain. Being simple-minded, he did not know that it was the king. "What ails you, friend?" he asked. "I'm thirsty," replied the king. So the fool took a cup from the bedside table, filled it with water, and gave it to the king. He drank, the wound was healed, and there in his hand was the Holy Grail. He turned to the fool and asked, "How could you find what my bravest and brightest could not?" And the fool replied, "I don't know. I only knew that you were thirsty."

LETTER THIRTEEN
All Saintstide to Advent 1992

These are dark days. It seems as if we are being led by the unswerving mercy of God into yet more darkness, led to a place where we can only wait in silence, immersed in the womb of an unborn age. Slowly the lights by which we used to find our way diminish and go out. One by one old certainties are challenged and fade. Words, themselves so often the bringers of light, appear and disappear like lightning, so soon are they used up and are no longer trustworthy.

Every day it seems as if we are a fragment of a jigsaw puzzle of a whole people struggling to be born. We are not yet ready, but we are thrust into the chaos of emerging from the womb. And that being born is happening not when or where or how we expected.

We are born each day into an ever more complex world, the reports of the roving media our daily bread. Give us this day our daily world. And the din crashes in: births, sorrows, ecstasies, horrors, deaths. The bells toll incessantly.

The whole frame groans and shudders. Something is going on much bigger than any one of us can experience, let alone understand. We hear only discords, and yet each phrase may be contributing to an overwhelming new harmonic. We have no choice but to be part of all this, responding to so many calls to live and die. Over and over again we feel sucked out, unprepared, threatened, engulfed by the blood and slime of what we cannot yet recognize as a new creation.

My own birth is enough to cope with – barely that, let alone be embroiled with all these others who impinge upon me. It is a paradox: unless we live with all the others we shall not properly survive our own daily being born.

So too it is necessary to return to the darkness, to be immersed in what is yet unborn. We have to come back from the edges where the splinters of light probe us and cut us. As mature human beings with some gift of wisdom, we are called to go deeper into the dark silence of our womb. Without doing this we cannot survive, we cannot act rightly, we cannot make our contribution to the survival and re-creation of the world.

It is a necessary part of our spiritual journey. We are to descend into the unborn place beneath the compulsions of our age, beneath our own compulsions, so that when we return we may have something to give in words and actions.

Darkness need not be blindness. It can be a way of seeing, a way of going forward. In the dark womb the one who is yet to be born can see with its whole being. There are no sounds, no lights, to distract. But in this adult coming to birth, we have to let go of so much as we descend, so as to be ready for our birth into each new day. We must make contact with the deep dark ground, the place where we can only receive. We have to give up giving out. We need to recover the sense that all is gift, all is of God. Without it we shall not survive.

Children in the womb are the constant recipients of the unknown. They are nurtured and transformed by what they receive, by what they do not know. So for us on our adult journey within. We reach down to the foundations of our being, soul deep, where we are laid out in silence, open to the transforming meeting with God, where the divine and human come together in an unexpected kiss.

Here, by giving away everything to the stillness and the silence we learn not only our own soul, but we meet the soul of the world, the soul of creation, from which we cannot be separated. We touch it and we know it. What may at first threaten to be the scream I cannot withstand turns into the most sublime calling note of all. This music truly is of God and each of us has carried it within since the moment of our conception. Here we are invited to rest with God beyond the constrictions of our time and space. This is where our ultimate hope rests, beyond everything we know ourselves to be. Here, all the time, we are being called beyond the known limits and being fed by what is beyond. The beyond comes in. So the darkness becomes the place where our sensitivity to the whole being of God increases. But we have to learn to give this space to God, whence all our meaning comes.

It is also an act of utter faith – nothing but faith, nothing else. There are no deals, no cut-price bargains, no haggling with words. All these have to be left behind. And without faith there is no answer to the question, What's the point?

To paraphrase Eckhart, to take silent leisure is more useful than many of our deeds. For Bede Griffiths, "Stillness within one individual can affect society beyond measure."

And it is not a choice between inaction and action, but of learning to be still *and* learning how to choose right action.

It is hard to accept this, that action without stillness may well be the wrong kind of action. It is indeed difficult to discipline the time for silence when the world is so insistent with its next round of urgencies. How to distinguish between what is urgent and what is important: that also needs wisdom.

Eckhart again: "Talking about God and putting it ahead of silence is a sin" because to be silent is to be with God. Silence is the assurance of God's presence, not absence. Silence is the dark faithfulness of God's promise. Talking puts distance between us, treats God as an object, as an 'out there', when, above all, we need to recover a sense of the presence of God who is within, and in whom we are enfolded. It is in St John's Gospel, chapter 17: you in me...I in you...they in us...I in them...you in me.

I believe that time in this dark silent place is not a luxury, not only for a retreat, not an occasional optional extra, but essential. It is to be like Mary, as it were womb within the womb of God, journeying day by day, and each day harder than the last, yet full of the one as yet unknown song.

It is this mystery that many thousands of the young have stumbled into through the discipline and faith of Taizé and have found themselves to be at home in such a darkness. Brother Roger said last Pentecost:

> As we grapple face to face with our unknown future, do not be afraid, do not lose heart. The past, your past, is enfolded in the heart of Jesus. Your future with God is certain. Do not be severe with yourself or with others. Rest in the joy of Jesus Christ.

PS. Oh dear, so many words about silence! I wish I could tell it with such direct wisdom as in this story told by Anthony de Mello, *The Song of the Bird*.

Kakua was the first Japanese to study Zen in China. He did not travel at all. He just meditated assiduously. Whenever people sought him and found him and asked him to preach, he would say a few words, and then move to another part of the forest where he was less likely to be found.

When he eventually returned to Japan, the Emperor heard of him and asked him to preach Zen for his benefit and that of the whole court. Kakua stood there in front of the Emperor in silence. Then he pulled out a flute from the folds of his robe and played a short note on it. He then bowed profoundly to the Emperor and disappeared.

LETTER FOURTEEN
Pentecost 1993

This letter has to be about hope. For we are supposed to be people of hope, those who reach out into hope beyond hope.

And we are plunged into the deepest darkness.

David Jenkins (at one time Bishop of Durham) warned of a sort of approaching doom, a dark night of the institutions. We have certainly come to it. International leaders, repeatedly overwhelmed by events, struggle valiantly with little notion of which way to turn, living at best day by day. They just keep on keeping on. The word 'evil' is on the lips of so many ordinary people, not simply those attempting to be theologians. People smell it, hear it, talk about it in day-to-day conversation. Wherever the eye looks, whether upon a two-year-old slaughtered child or a once beautiful holiday resort in ruins, the seeing is withered. Look again, and famine feasts upon you like a plague of leeches. People are horrified by decay and putrefaction. This is an age of darkness so long foreseen. In every direction there is holocaust, innocent sacrifices burning in the darkness. And it is dark.

It is almost too easy to write about. It sounds melodramatic. The words slide glibly on the page. But this darkness is real. We have to embrace it, go into this abyss where everything burns in the darkness, being prepared to go down far, far beyond the point that human strength can take us or allow us to go.

In the heart of the abyss is the gaze of God. We have to believe that is so: it is our only hope. At the point of the most terrible suffering the gaze of God is waiting for us to be there to return the gaze and live the mystery. Who can bear it?

No attempt at an explanation can give any satisfaction. Perhaps my words pander to my pomposity. Perhaps I should leave this page blank with only the words: Let the reader understand. Job says: "I have spoken of things which I have not understood." And he yields to the dust and ashes. Yet this has to be where the

Promise actually is. We have to go into it, immerse ourselves in it, not stand by simply looking. Sacrifices have to be offered in compassion, alongside those countless innocents who cannot escape, who are thrown into the abyss every day. To choose to move into the heart of the abyss, to dwell there, is what is asked of us if we are to draw near to the God who has chosen to stand by abused creation and share all its experience.

And again: what dramatic pulp, what heroic claptrap. Yet it is so.

To plunge into the darkness constantly involves leaving everything behind, becoming empty and destitute of human resource, and casting ourselves into the appalling mercy of God in the heart of the darkness. Even a leap down as a momentary brilliant explosion of sacrifice seems little, for the sparks are snuffed out and muffled into nothing in the darkness. There are no words to guide or act as helpmeets. It is a total silence, for ever black, down, black, down. There is nothing there but the waiting in hope, the hope of God's Promise. It is only from God, there, that we can dare to take hope.

To be still and silent and waiting in prayer: this is what we are called to. It cuts through the machine gun clatter of media and politics, with all their distortions, and through the wailing prophets on every street corner who are too ready to lay blame and find scapegoats.

The final response is to fall silent before what we strive to understand and never can, except without words. The action of being there as ourselves speaks a greater word than all our mouthing.

And from that awful place something new begins to happen, a new beauty and purity are created. The gaze of God can meet the violence and horror, never extinguished by them, always creating something new. And we are called to be co-creators with the Christ for whom death and resurrection are inseparable. And we have to participate in that place where these things happen in and through us. We take our part in the 'the fellowship of his sufferings'. "You shall be a crown of beauty in the hand of the Lord, and a royal diadem in the hand of your God." (Isaiah 62.3)

At that still point of helplessness where all has been burned away by this terrible darkness, we are to be the small bearers of the beauty of God. Part of the sacrifice that we make is that we shall never know that this is happening, we can only trust that it is so, and be content with that. For once we become aware that in returning gaze for gaze we have become the eye of God's recreating beauty and purity, inevitably as human beings with our limitations we start to diffuse it and corrupt it.

A story:

> Buddha's disciple Subhuti suddenly discovered how rich emptiness is. The realization that the best way to live is to hold on to nothing and let the self be empty. For everything, every moment, every relationship passes, is impermanent. In this moment of divine emptiness he sat in bliss under a tree when suddenly flowers began to fall all around him. And the gods whispered, "We are enraptured by your sublime teachings on emptiness." Subhuti replied, "But I haven't uttered a word about emptiness." "True," the gods replied, "You have not spoken of emptiness, we have not heard of emptiness. This is true emptiness." And the shower of blossoms continued to fall.

If I spoke of my emptiness, or was even aware of it, would it be emptiness? Music needs the hollowness of the flute, letters the blankness of the page, light the void called a window, God the absence of self at the heart of self.

LETTER FIFTEEN
All Saintstide to Advent 1993

It has been the most beautiful autumn in Cumbria, with weeks of virtually no rain and the colours everywhere ablaze. Everything is fragile, dying, waiting. The wind will be the hinge of the seasons and suddenly all will drop into the bareness of winter.

The roads and scuffling footpaths will flow red.

Somehow, with so much beauty in death, it is easier to believe in the promise of God that all shall be well, even against the human backcloth stained with so many other reds. But how can we express the promise in these massacred days when so many feel that everything is out of control and the world is falling apart?

There do not even seem to be any innocent games any more, our children's eyes screwed into the violent fantasies of the video screen. Repeated violence scrambles the brain: or is it only a game?

Can we still ride our surfboards through the crashing waves, the swell getting more and more powerful? Keep your balance and ride in, eyes on the shore. The promise is contained in the falling. Change the metaphor and think of the shell splintering into a thousand pieces to disclose the nut, which is not enough to satisfy the appetite but may take the edge off the hunger.

Faith has to say that this is all part of the process of a new creation. It is threatening, it is bloody, it is dark. If we felt we were in control it would not be dark. The mystic invites us to receive a ray of divine darkness. For God is beyond the light and can ultimately be known only in darkness. Even if the mayhem lasts through generations, we have continually to hand ourselves over to the Spirit of God, again and again restoring our sense of wonder and dark mystery. Materialism, where everything is measured and discarded by the criterion of usefulness and where the ego-self rules, has to career on to its ferocious end. To value the material is fine in its place, but it has grown out of all proportion and the philosophy has become demonic. In spasms of increasing violence it thrashes its way to its end.

Yet, here and there are spaces between the violence, something quite new is beginning to happen in the life of humankind. It is pushing past those things which have to fall apart to make way for what is to come. Change the picture again: the human mind is pressed into the nose cone of a spacecraft and the booster rockets fall away to leave it weightless and bewildered and wondering where it is headed.

Bede Griffiths died in May this year. He was a Benedictine monk who spent the last forty years of his life in an ashram in India, stretching out his arms to hold and draw together the spiritualities of East and West. He said it was like bringing together the two halves of his own soul. His life was based on deep daily meditation, waiting in silence in the presence of God, opening his spirit to God's Spirit.

He gave us a new vision of reality.

> The heaven and the earth which we experience through our limited mental consciousness is only a passing phenomenon. We are destined to pass beyond our present levels of consciousness where we see everything in terms of dualities, of subject and object, time and space, heaven and earth, and to enter into the unifying consciousness beyond the dualities of the mind.

This is the heavenly country towards which we are travelling. Bede Griffiths finds one of his strongest allies in modern physics where everything is seen to be part of everything else. The explosion of matter in the universe fifteen billion years ago is present to all of us now.

In the beginning, well almost, matter was created. Matter gave birth to consciousness and began to be transfigured. The process continues as consciousness grows, all the time transforming matter. In Jesus it finally takes possession of matter and matter starts to become spiritualized, divinized. Matter becomes transfigured into cosmic consciousness.

We are caught up in this immense process, towards a total awareness of the harmony of all things. It will not be the original undifferentiated union but a harmony in which everything preserves its uniqueness and yet is held together. We with God will be doing the holding. The cosmic consciousness is God's gift to us.

It brings a new dimension to the prayer in the Gospel according to John, chapter 17: May they be one in us as you are in me and I am in you...with me in them and you in me, may they be so completely one that this world will realize...

This is what is coming, this is what we are beginning to live. Fully to realize it is bound to be costly, as agonizing as the agony of Jesus, which we are invited to share, moving towards unity in God's love. We cannot stop it but we can delay it. We can turn aside and ignore it, as materialism invites us to. But the greater invitation is to enter the darkness, even the sense of catastrophe and failure, not knowing when all the sufferings will be complete. We know only the promise that we shall be like the divine and see God as we have never yet seen.

God is asking us to wait, here and now, still and empty, so that through us and unknown by us the Holy Spirit of God may pour the more fully into the new creation. We do not and cannot understand this. We cannot make sense of it, make it plain, however much it is important to try. We can but live it in faith.

I met a Lutheran pastor once in East Germany in the days of the Berlin Wall. He had lived in Eisenach since 1945. It was the town where Bach was born in 1685 and where the Bach family made music in the principal church for a hundred and sixty years. Above the town rises the Wartburg and its castle where Luther took refuge in the sixteenth century. Preparations were in hand to celebrate the fifth centenary of the reformer's birth. As we walked through the warm and dingy town the pastor said, "Communism is like topsoil over the deep loam of our history. It is all there underneath. The only problem is: it's my lifetime."

LETTER SIXTEEN
Pentecost 1994

This gift of darkness, dear friends: it is to become more and more aware that to live in darkness for the rest of our lives is a gift. That passage from Isaiah that heralds Christmas for us and begins, "The people that walked in darkness..." – that's us.

Why is Nelson Mandela such a sign of hope? It is because he has lived in the heart of this present darkness for twenty-seven years and allowed it to become a gift. He disappeared from human view, stripped to nothing of all those things that most of us depend on. All his illusions, all his false gods: gone. With constant discipline he allowed himself to be purified by the severities imposed on him, leaving him ready for nothing but justice, forgiveness, reconciliation. He is man come of age who is living out of the truth that there is no way of going forward but together. He had no choice, the circumstances were forced upon him. In some measure, we are called to choose it.

And this darkness we are being called to embrace is indeed about coming of age, about receiving the divine ray hidden in the heart of the darkness. Mandela has shown us what we have to do – and that is not eulogy, simply description. This present darkness is a call to be purified. We have to be content to be disillusioned with all things in order to receive the gift of radical clarity. The darkness of despair which begins now to cloak every form of visible life in our civilization is the beginning of wisdom because it purges us of all false hope and begins the journey into reality, into what it means to be a real human being made in the image of God. We are being called forward into joy.

Fantasies have too long fandangoed before our greedy eyes, feeding only our dissatisfactions and increasingly separating us from one another. Everything flies apart. We have perverted our religions into cooking pots of hunger to appease, thirsts to assuage. We have tied into them our personal systems of tithes and rewards, a myriad of little fixes and tricks and concealments. As Bede Griffiths put it, "Religions have in turn become fossilized and have to be renewed, not only in themselves but also in relation to one another."

So personally and as a civilization we tumble down through repeated disappointments until we arrive at the black hole where truth begins. Who can face entering this black hole and joining by choice the many Mandelas of this world who are already submerged, becoming even more vulnerable to the hostile forces present in the darkness? It is not easy, there are no shortcuts. Yet it *is* a divine gift.

This letter is a reminder, first to myself, of this invitation to enter into dark prayer. The Community of the Three Hours is a reminder of the dark wordless prayer of the Good Friday Christ, and of the requirement, somewhere in our living, to make a sacrifice that deliberately demolishes our expectations. What I suppose I seek is the setting aside of time for dead-to-all-we-know prayer, dead-of-night prayer, the dark silent prayer where we have to learn the discipline of passing through the laser beams of a thousand distractions. This is 'useless' prayer rather than the 'worthwhile' kind of prayer where there is an end product, an act of worship, a satisfaction of words gone through and completed to the best of our ability (which may also be part of what we have to do).

This is slow prayer, surrendering 'doing' prayer to 'being' prayer. Each time is a new beginning because it is dark. There are no grades, no achievements. To be there is about creating space in the darkness. Indeed, we create it by being there. We make space for the coming things of God to grow. Whenever we create we have to make space, and that slows up everything and changes our expectations. We give up the space – for the garden to be planted, for the bookcase to be made, for the child to be born, for the wound to heal. We have to make space if things are to be brought together. And this creates community.

How many aeons of time did it take for H_2 to join with O and become water? For the cells of my skin to become flesh? How many millions of disney-like life frames were needed to perfect the simple gesture of raising a hand in greeting? We are an early people on an immense journey. There is no quick and easy way for things to come together. It needs much 'useless' time. So dark prayer is slow prayer, and we have to 'will' the space for God's growing.

One elderly holy friend describes it as the "apostolate of just being there", and if you create the space, "people come and openings are made."

Another believes that to offer this dark prayer against the asphyxiating pressures of the times is one of the most profound services anyone can render to humanity.

A third says that descending constantly into this discipline in her daily life has opened her out into a new sense of wonder at God's presence in all things.

Mandela has never lost his vision that the land could be beautiful. In *all* things God is waiting only to surprise us with joy. In the dark silence we are caught up in the making of a new world.

Here is a meditation I heard recently on Silence:

> Place my mouth into your custody, my Lord,
> look after my lips.   PSALM 141.3
>
> But Jesus held his silence.   MATTHEW 26.63

Silence is gentleness.
When you don't react against offences,
when you don't claim your rights,
when you let God defend your honour,
        silence is gentleness.

Silence is mercy.
When you don't reveal another's faults,
when you forgive without searching into the past,
when you don't condemn but intercede with all your heart,
        silence is mercy.

Silence is patience.
When you suffer without complaining,
when you don't search for the comfort of others,
when you don't interfere but wait for the seed to sprout slowly,
        silence is patience.

Silence is humility.
When you keep silent to let your brother emerge,
when you hide God's gifts in your discretion,
when you let your behaviour be misunderstood,
when you leave the glory of the enterprise to others,
        silence is humility.

Silence is faith.
When you keep silent because it's God who acts,
when you renounce the sounds and voices of the world to stay
                           with God,
when you don't search for sympathy because you are satisfied
                    with being known by God,
        silence is faith.

Silence is worship.
When you embrace sacrifice without asking Why?
        silence is worship.

LETTER SEVENTEEN
All Saintstide to Advent 1994

All Saintstide is about our travelling in communion with all other people, and it is about smallness.

The saints are those who know that they are small. We are called to know that at heart we are utterly dependent and helpless, to sense at every membrane our fragile and fragmentary place in the scheme of things. However long we live, whatever we do, our own moment is infinitesimally small.

Of course we can seem very large, by the accumulation of each and every footstep and impression – and each of these is in itself precious. We may even pursue a grand design for our lives, or have one mapped out for us, even if we are only vaguely aware of it. But the bigger we get, the more lights around our name, the more letters and phone calls and visitors, the more we become caught, the more our lives become drudgery, evened out into inescapable routines. So it is all the more important to return again and again to our one small place of prayer – and to be completely and unerringly disciplined about it.

Of course each and every minute step is also precious. And it is a saving grace to pass things on and, more important, to let things pass through us, to recognize that each moment is significant, but not to cling to it. Each gift received and each gift passed on is for our humbling. And in this smallness, this lowliness, we are given the freedom of our unique contribution to the scheme of things.

Over-heavy, we lumber around with everything out of proportion. Overfed, we waddle and wander without direction, without poise, in the end collapsing into inertia. Slimmed down we become more alert, more poised, more recollected and centred. We become aware of the wonder of existence, attentive to it, responding to it.

When we are small, we are more able to be attentive to others, waiting with them or for them. We may at times feel impatient and useless, but we stay there, waiting, even if we don't know where they are. The temptation is to come to premature conclusions and rush on. One of the ancients said that it is the madman who is breathless.

It is a gift to us when others will wait with us for as long as we need: the parent waiting for the toddler to catch up; the teacher who does not tut-tut over our inability to grasp something; the one who waits to welcome you when you return, either the prodigal or the last in the race.

The call to prayer is to become small, to wait in the small, centred space, and it will dawn upon us that here is the place where everything and everyone *is*. Here, where we encounter 'people and realms of every tongue', we meet and share our common dependency and helplessness. Small calls to small beneath the roar of the waters. To enter this prayer is to be willing to engage in the giving and receiving of 'smallnesses', to acknowledge that by myself I can do nothing. Such waiting acknowledges that I do not know how to pray at all, and I can but be silent in the presence of others. We approach the needle's eye that we are all called to be threaded through. It is the heart of prayer.

It is not easy. To be small, to wait, simply to be silent at the point of interchange, is also to dwell in deep darkness. It is the void, the point of emptiness. And we do not know how long we will have to wait. We cannot put a time limit on it, as if we were standing on a platform between trains and looking at our watch. But if we are rash and wasteful in the time we give to the waiting, even to the enduring of an agony – "Take this cup from me" – we may come to the place where we realize that we know our own uniqueness and also our belonging to everything and everyone else.

Remember in Advent, Mary, waiting, heavy, content to wait with God, at another's pace and not her own.

So it is that holiness is created through us and in us, it is then that the unknown begins to break through, that we start to recognize the impossibilities which are after all possible, to feel way beyond our bones the heaving tilt in the axis of the earth towards divine life.

John McCarthy's five hostage years of waiting in Beirut, of learning to be small, are almost history. In *Some Other Rainbow* Jill Morrell reflects: "My vision seemed to have been blurred by having too much to look at, whereas his had been sharpened by having so little."

I am also indebted to them for this poem 'Wait for me' by the Russian poet Konstantina Simonov:

> Wait for me and I'll return.
> Only wait very hard,
> Wait when you are filled with sorrow
> As you watch the yellow rain,
> Wait when the winds sweep the snowdrifts,
> Wait in the weltering heat,
> Wait when others have stopped waiting,
> Forgetting their yesterdays.
> Wait even when from afar no letters come to you,
> Wait even when others are tired of waiting
> And friends sit around the fire,
> Drinking to my memory,
> Wait, and do not hurry to drink to my memory too.

Wait. For I'll return, defying every death.
And let those who do not wait say that I was lucky.
They will never understand that in the midst of death,
You with your waiting saved me.
Only you and I now know I survived.
It's because you waited as no-one else did.

Lastly, this piece from *Encounter*, a publication of the USPG:

"Large parts of Lake Victoria have been declared a disaster area because of thousands of bodies washed down from the civil war in Rwanda." This was the opening headline of tonight's evening news, a gruesome reminder in the litany of humanity's inhumanity. By the time these words are read there will have been other atrocities, whose obscenity will have tempted us to despair and make us wonder whether prayer is anything more than a comfort blanket in the encroaching darkness.

Often when I think like this my mind goes to some words of Walter Wink: "We are not easily reduced to prayer. We who grope toward praying today are like a city gutted by fire. Those who pray do so not because they believe certain intellectual propositions about the value of prayer, but simply because the struggle to be human in the face of suprahuman powers requires it. Intercession is spiritual defiance of what is, in the name of what God has promised."

LETTER EIGHTEEN
Days after Pentecost 1995

"Everything on the way to heaven is heaven," says Catherine of Siena. And John Main wrote, "The Kingdom is not a place we are going to but rather an experience we carry with us on every breath." How can we live as if eternity is here and now whilst at the same time allowing our innermost recesses to be open to the never-ending tide of human misery and, as Charles Péguy put it, "receive the evil at its greatest stress"?

How can I live as if the whole of *my* living is the sum of my attempts to put the key I have been given into the eternal door and be continually opening it so that time, my time, loses the restricting frame in which it holds me, and becomes steeped in eternity? For there is only one life really, eternal life, always here. Can I live with eternity as *the* reality, not time, without losing contact with human endeavour and suffering? It is far from easy to make of such sufferings a springboard rather than a quagmire.

Robert is living with decay and destruction all around him. It is the inner city story where so much is crumbling. It is his job, his life, his passion, to be there. He calls it living in the dragon's mouth, living with the dark face of God. He has to be like a solitary miner's lamp lowering himself down into the acrid black tunnels of a pit disaster. And yet – everything on the way to heaven is heaven.

Komadi, a Japanese poet, writes: "It is because we are in Paradise that all things in the world wrong us. When we go out from Paradise, nothing hurts us, nothing matters."

When we are given this key, put into our hands, to live in "the terrible beauty when things fall apart", in Brian Keenan's vivid words, we have to learn at every moment to keep on recovering wonder, love, and praise. While being staggered by the world's loss, I have equally to descend to the same place within, in the faith that it is precisely there that I shall discover the gateway of praise where the song is forever sung.

To do that I have to become smaller, ever smaller, leaving on the surface all measures of time, to let them go, with all their associated judgments, qualifications, gifts, experience, achieve-ments, status, demands, expectations, failures – all of it. To live the eternal while being bound by time: it demands that we are cleaned out of everything save adoration and love. And that is how I have to live.

For the door does then swing open into the intricate wonder of being alive at all. I am alive! I am alive! And the more I gasp in adoration the more I discover that "victory suddenly appears in the hour of defeat." (Thomas Merton) However constantly I feel pressed to separate time and eternal life, just as constantly I am called to refuse to do so.

Etty, in the concentration camp in 1942–3, facing the horrors, can still say (coming to my rescue): "What matters is the richness of your inner life, not whether you are inside or outside the prison camp." Addressing God, she says, "Your dwelling place is within us to the last."

It is part of the life of prayer to be steadfastly and frequently disciplined to descend again and again deep within, and to be there, and to be still, and to be empty. Unless we offer ourselves into this stillness we never meet ourselves as we really are, that is, in God. We never arrive because we are for ever taking our leave, moving on, always restless. (The mind that is too active ends up by not being a mind at all.)

Of course it takes courage to do this, for it implies learning, slowly and painfully, to destroy in ourselves what our ego selves seek to destroy in others.

But as we persist we find something happening that seems extraordinary. Miracles of love start to unfold in daily life, or perhaps we start to notice what was already there but we didn't see them. People change before our eyes. They look different. And they draw us into deeper suffering: as love grows, so does solidarity. Adoration and suffering, love and pain: they belong together. 'Miracles' and 'crucifixion' cannot be separated. This also is heaven.

This waiting in stillness is not only for our sake. It is creation's hope. Meister Eckhart wrote: "Nothing in all creation is so like God as stillness." We are called to live as exactly *there* as we can, so that those "who come after us do not have to start again…To be a centre of peace in the madhouse changes the madhouse." (Etty)

I received this in response to these letters from one who is older and wiser than I as she spends her life balanced now between waiting in prayer and waiting on others.

What I ask is not great putting out to sea
Or even being busy in home waters.
But – 'steady as she goes' –
Prayerfully, vigilantly, expectantly,
Helping to sweep the jetsam and the mines
From before the path
Of frailer vessels, while they too become
Seasoned for travel.

FRANCES WILKINSON

And this: remember that nightingales sing in the dark...

LETTER NINETEEN
Advent 1995

The commitment to praying the Three Hours each Friday has first and foremost been a gift of the Spirit to me. Since it became clear that it was right to practise it, my life has changed immeasurably. The whole week somehow revolves around it. I can't quantify that 'immeasurably'. I can't even say that there is much to show for it. It is like a river flowing through the countryside where the landscape would be so different if it wasn't there. And this seems to be true for others as well as for me.

At this moment though I feel blank. I am in one of those moods where I look at the Church, without which I would be nothing, and think: it is so hard to love it. I suppose I want it to slow down, to be less like trains that never stop to let people get on. Worship is hectic rather than unhurried. Church members seem frenetic and increasingly driven. If it would only slow down I feel sure people would be drawn into its life more. There is this terrible pressure to keep everything going, holding on when the need is to let go. If only we could all stop and be silent and delve deep, far away from the agitating waves caused by expectations and targets and performance. We are giving birth out of the top of our heads, and so giving birth to no new thing, only the repetitions of our tired minds. We need to be in the belly of the Spirit for something real to be born.

In the Gospels we see Jesus' 'economy' of time and energy, the right action proceeding from a deep stillness and silence. People of other faiths seem to know this better than Christians do. If only we could stop, listen, do less, simply be, and quietly wait.

Now I am not very good at this prayer of the Three Hours. 'Faithful' is perhaps a better word, being faithful to the gift – and that is what I'm not very good at. It is often boring and monotonous, and sleep keeps nudging in from the sidelines. But one of the fruits has been to become aware that all kinds of 'miracles' are happening, even if I don't exactly know what they are, nor do I need or want to know. It's rather that in odd moments there is a kind of microflash, instantaneous, gone almost immediately, and yet something whole and complete is given. It is more like the splutter of an old car engine on a cold morning. But it is real. I don't know when it is coming and where it is coming from, and I certainly couldn't predict it.

I suppose I long for the whole Church to be suffused with this sense of miracle and wonder. If only we could live the mystery of the Church's wisdom, arising from the dark and silent catacombs of our own deepest silence and love.

There comes the moment when we simply *know* that old priorities have to shift. This may go against our particular grain, facing us with alarming decisions. Yet we know. It is a call to the desert rather than the market place, the wilderness rather than the shopping mall.

Kosuke Koyama, a Japanese Christian, preached a sermon called 'Three mile an hour God'. In it he reckons God took his people into the wilderness to learn one lesson, that human beings do not live by bread alone – and it took a very long time, 'forty' years. "Isn't this a rather slow and costly way for God to let his people know…?" They were taught the truth, Koyama says, as they walked, at three miles an hour, led by this three miles an hour

God. God walks slowly because he is love. If he were not love he would have moved much faster. Love has its own speed, "It is an inner speed...It is 'slow', yet it is lord over all other speeds since it is the speed of love, the speed of the promise of God."

It is so hard to get the balance right, between inner and outer. A local vicar of great secular abilities and experience has recently decided that for the next eighteen months he will simply stay in his small rural parish and refuse all invitations to do anything at all outside it. He intends to be there and to *attend* – slowly and deeply to prayer and to the life around him.

Are the thoughts in this newsletter merely the vague meanderings of a weary soul no longer in the mainstream of life, or are they the pain of an ageing eager man who feels as if he is only just beginning? I would of course like to think that it is the second! Perhaps some words of others will help to expand the things of the spirit that are underneath my own words.

> I stepped down into the most hidden depth of my being, lamp in hand and ears alert, to discover whether in the deepest recesses of the blackness within me I might not see the glint of the waters of the current that flows on, whether I might not hear the murmur of the mysterious waters that rise from the uttermost depths, and will burst forth no one knows where. With terror and intoxicating emotion I realized that my poor trifling existence was one with the immensity of all that is and all that is in the process of becoming.
>
> PIERRE TEILHARD DE CHARDIN
> *The Hymn of the Universe*

Silence is the doorway into the need of the world, the condition of the prayer which arises out of the heart of the universe, because it expresses the love of Christ, crucified and risen for the world. Such profound prayer, however, is not concerned only with the world as a whole, but also with the most mundane details of our ordinary everyday lives. Prayer is not a part-time occupation, and there can no more be part-time contemplatives than there can be part-time Christians. Without the contemplative dimension in our lives, we cannot be fully human. This contemplative dimension is the fruit of our willingness to meet the discipline of learning to wait in silence and stillness, as well as the boredom and loneliness and sometimes the apparent emptiness which confront us in the waiting. Contemplation and action are both necessary to basic stability. There is need to take regular times of quiet in order to be disciplined in the generous giving of self in our activity.

MOTHER MARY CLARE
Encountering the Depths

LETTER TWENTY
Days after Pentecost 1996

It is so hard really to live from the 'poor' place within. We seek to compensate by indulging in fits of extravagance: the night out that costs too much, the extra clothes or holiday we can't afford, the top-of-the-range luxury, the hang it, what the hell. And what is your binge?

Where is the mood of extravagance towards our times of prayer, the daily and weekly giving what we feel we cannot afford? Not for the hell of it but for the inescapable heaven that we always keep at arm's length. There is, after all, so much to do...

Perhaps the Three Hours is a 'minder' − or a reminder that we have to be extravagant in this movement inward. It is the extravagance of constantly returning to the central stillness, to the emptying place where we hold on to nothing. It is a *painstaking* silence.

It is easier to get people to serve on a committee than to pray in church... The pressure is always there for us to fit in, the ego whispering to us that it is a waste to be so extravagant of our time: better to get involved, stay in control, keep your head above water.

We are always hearing the cry that prayer is being squeezed out, yet this being with God is what set us going in the first place.

It is only with such extravagance that we can learn to recognize the pressures that the ego exerts upon us, and to let them go – again and again. Instead of doing we have to be undone. Tired out from playing all the games of the ego, we have to allow ourselves to be unbuttoned slowly and quietly by the waiting parent. We need to take the time to loosen our hold, to stop grasping, to be the object of another's attention, to be done to. It is part of prayer to run like a child into the mother's lap.

Buddhists say that to pray is to practise death in order to be fully alive. Waiting becomes rich with expectancy rather than empty with desolation, and our dying times in all their variety become triumphs rather than defeats. To be extravagant in the practice of prayer is to descend more deeply than we ever thought possible into the knowledge that everybody else is dying too. This realization can bring us totally to life, evoking compassion because we have entered into the hearts of others.

This kind of self-knowledge is crucial. The only way to truth is through ourselves – though not the self of the credit cards, the identifying numbers, the proofs of who we are. I love the story of the Zen monk who goes into the bank and is asked for evidence of his identity. He asked the teller for a mirror, looked into it, and said happily, "Yes, it's me all right."

Richard Rohr writes:

> Ego takes endless disguises…and is dominating so many of the institutions of the Church…It remains largely out of control. Gospel people don't need to hang on to anything. For them, the ego is out of the way. They'll make a difference in the world precisely because they don't need to. They don't need to be first, they don't need to be important, they don't need to be number one. They don't need to be rich, secure, popular: they can do what God has told them to do. They can be obedient, God can move through them with power. That's why spirituality is always about letting go.

There is much valuable territory to journey through on the road to self-knowledge: good processes of learning, various therapies, counselling, psychoanalysis, and other disciplines. In the end though the paradox remains that we become more self-conscious, more ego-aware, only so that we can give it all away, becoming less self-conscious, getting ourselves out of the way, no longer centre stage. To let go of everything we have painfully and joyfully learned about ourselves is the only way we can truly know ourselves. We have to go into a black hole of utterly empty and silent prayer given to the God whose Word came out of such silence.

To be extravagant with the stillness and the silence, to be extravagant in a willingness to enter the dark and stay there: it is like finding a baby on a battlefield and simply staying there to babysit. No wonder we try and run away.

We live in an 'end-of-the-age' time. We are overloaded with information. We are bewildered by the accelerating rate of change. We retire and we find we are busier than ever. And we place ourselves in the Three Hours, extravagantly slow, ready to enter the dark, the unknown, the silence, prepared to be an exile, a wanderer, a stranger in a foreign land.

And we discover there the Jesus of the Cross who is a kind of scarecrow, a black figure scaring away all that would hinder the growth of what is true in the soil of our lives. He hangs there, an exile in his own land, "singing the Lord's song in a strange land", creating a new beauty in the darkness, "what eye has not seen nor heart conceived". The heart's darkness is the place where the sun rises.

> To discover God
> is not to discover an idea
> but to discover oneself.
> It is to awaken
> to that part of one's existence
> which has been hidden from sight
> and which one has refused to recognize.

The discovery may be very painful;
it is like going through
a kind of death.

But it is the one thing
which makes life
worth living.

BEDE GRIFFITHS

Central silence is there:
no creature may enter, nor any idea,
there the soul neither thinks nor acts
nor entertains any idea,
either of itself or anything else.

MEISTER ECKHART

The father uttered one word;
that word is his son,
and he utters him for ever in everlasting silence;
and in silence the soul has to hear it.

JOHN OF THE CROSS

Above all, trust in the slow work of God. We are, quite naturally,
impatient in everything to reach the end without delay. We should
like to skip the intermediate stages. We are impatient of being on
the way to something unknown, something new, and yet it is the
law of all progress that it is made by passing through some stages
of instability – and that it may take a very long time.

PIERRE TEILHARD DE CHARDIN

LETTER TWENTY-ONE
All Saints to Advent 1996

This letter is about despair and celebrates those who live it. It is a salute to trusted friends who have long dwelt in darkness without seeing any great light.

The road from All Saints at the beginning of November to Advent at the end of November is short, straight, and inescapable. If you aspire to saintliness, letting the perfection of the divinity grow in you (though you will not recognize it when it comes!), then you have to accept the uncomfortable gifts that Advent offers: not gold, frankincense, and myrrh, but waiting, despair, judgment. The saintly road is not so much about striving to pull up holy socks as letting them slide down. Not that you sag in holiness, but we are asked to adopt a discipline of surrender. Advent is about learning to surrender. It is about surrendering everything that we hold on to, aware of our huge attachments and passing judgment on them by letting them go.

Advent, the season of hope, can so readily become the quick fix season of false hopes. We like the Advent candles, we like the illuminated crib, but we whizz through the intervening darkness trying to bypass the tollgate of despair, filled only with the sound of our own heavy breathing as we exhaust ourselves towards Christmas. It's fast lane stuff, and you try waiting in the fast lane! There is no true hope without despair and the crucial judgments that accompany it.

The Church is for the most part in the fast lane, being driven harder than it can faithfully go. It is hyperactive with false hope. It has to learn to recognize this. I once heard an Advent sermon which suggested that above the doorway of every church should be inscribed the text, "Abandon hope all ye who enter here." Rather, all ye who would enter sainthood let your socks down. The call to saintliness is to the discipline of surrendering our false hopes, every single thing that we might pin our hopes on.

We have to unclutch the grasping hand, to become, as the Buddhists say, totally unsticky. Every single hope we have is something *we* have made a picture of and that *we* are aiming to make come true. God, however, is totally out of the frame of all such pictures.

In the days when we didn't talk about hysterectomies women would whisper to one another about a neighbour in hospital for a certain operation, "She's had it all taken away." To enter an empty place of waiting where everything has been taken away is to begin to know despair. Strategies and beliefs don't work any more. It is the end of every illusion. The lights have gone out. It is indeed night.

We may do all that we can to scrabble away from this place, but the path toward sainthood leads us here sooner or later. We don't need any self-imposed austerities or hard lashings of fasting. We have simply to be steadfast in our waiting, and allow the bore- dom to happen, and the terrifying dispossession as one by one the things which others still seem to value and be inspired by, disap- pear. We have to wait with the utmost gentleness and yet with the utmost persistence, living both at once. This is the heart of our call. We have to learn to say, "This is the Lord's doing, and it is marvellous in our eyes."

I celebrate these friends who live most of their days in and out of the makeshifts of despair. The God the Church gave them has 'let them down'. They are still exhorted to 'play the game', but they find they are immobilised if they try follow the rules. Only by waiting constantly in the darkness do they discover that little by little they can move freely and with grace. Mostly, they still gather in awe round the common bread and wine, yet knowing that for them to continue to respond to that invitation is to take the taste of darkness into their mouths and return down their unlit mineshaft.

Some of their despair is born of their compassion for a world which, desperately hungry, turns for food to the Church, only to find that much of what is offered is long past its sell-by date. Nevertheless, blitz-worn as they are, they doggedly remain within the institution, moving amongst the rubble of its crumbling structures, quietly lifting up survivors.

They teach me that such dismay is a necessary gift on the road to the coming of God. It is the keenest cutting tool. It hones away, stripping the very tissue on which we thought our lives depended. It bares to the bone. How hard it is, at that waiting place, to have any faith that you are nearer to God than when you first believed.

But they are not gloomy people. To be true to what they see (rather, to what they do not see), they have had to let go of so much that there is a lightness about their step. Their disability has become their strength. They are alert and aware of the goodness of the world on their doorstep, of the presence of the divine nature, not to be eradicated, in every blaspheming soul. They bring clear air, clarity of vision – often unacceptable – to the Church they still love. The more they live in the faith of despair, the more it becomes a friendly giant. The deeper its emptiness the more daring and resilient they become. They are often prepared to accept that all things which reveal the absence of God are simply signs of presence. The emptiness is itself a language which somehow says, "Here I AM."

The barriers have come down for them. No longer is it easy to distinguish between enemy and friend. They are so poor that they need so little in order to celebrate. Filled with the sadness of human suffering, they can leap up in a moment, showering fun with divine irreverence.

Their company cheers me through the Church's seasons. They have put on the mantle of saintliness. Be sure to keep them, and one another, in your prayer's mind.

This meditation was used recently by the Dalai Lama at a predominantly Christian gathering. In all the bitterness of the banishment of Buddhism from Tibet it seems a fitting prayer for the Christmas child crucified.

> Regarding all sentient beings
> As excelling even the wish-granting gem
> For accomplishing the highest aim,
> May I always hold them most dear.

When in the company of others
I shall always consider myself the lowest of all,
And from the depth of my heart
Hold them dear and supreme.

Vigilant, the moment a delusion appears,
Which endangers myself and others,
I shall confront and avert it
Without delay.

When I see beings of wicked nature
Overwhelmed by violent negative actions and suffering,
I shall hold such rare ones dear,
As if I have found a precious treasure.

When someone I have benefited
And in whom I have great hopes
Gives me terrible harm,
I shall regard him as my holy spiritual friend.

In short, both directly and indirectly, do I offer
Every benefit and happiness to all sentient beings, my mothers;
May I secretly take on myself
All their harmful actions and sufferings.

May they not be defiled by the concepts
Of the eight profane concerns,
And aware that all things are illusory,
May they, ungrasping, be freed from bondage

LETTER TWENTY-TWO
Pentecost 1997

Anthony de Mello is a good friend of those for whom the Three Hours has some attraction and direction. *The Way of Love* is his last series of meditations. He reminds us that love is about learning to *see*, to see others as they really are, not as we think they are through our perpetual haze of conditioning and prejudice. We so rarely meet people with moment to moment freshness, on their terms rather than on our own. We are like a pilot who decides whether or not to fly today on the basis of last week's weather forecast. "The most painful act is the act of seeing. But it is in the act of seeing that love is born."

On the cross everything is bleakly clear. Jesus sees through everything because everything that might have clouded his perception, his vision of truth, the divinity at the heart of his being, has been taken away. All has gone: pictures about himself that others presented him with, all the special pleadings of approval and appreciation, illusions to do with friendship and loyalty, the supposed goodness of religion, mercy from opponents. It is a useless waste, a useless waiting, confusion, bewilderment, dark pain. "To love is to die to the need for persons and to be utterly alone." It has meaning only afterwards, and then only to some.

Such seeing is adoration. So the Three Hours is about seeing with this third eye, beyond physical sight and beyond the eye of the mind and the imagination. It is that waiting in stillness until the muddied water clears and we start seeing into the depths everything that is waiting to be seen.

Francis Dewar says this:

> God's primary calling to us is to be with him, to spend time in his presence, not as a means to something else, but simply because he is God and because we are made for relationship with him...Prayer is in the end totally useless and utterly important.

It is what we are made for and is absolutely no use for anything else.

The Three Hours, however it is observed, is a discipline about stopping. It is a decisive action. For me it seems to be utterly important to act in some such way in order to contradict the over-rationalizing, utilitarian nature of the culture in which I am trapped. What does it profit a man to gain access to the whole Internet and lose the way to his own soul? I still spend much of my time grading people, by their dress, posture, colour, language. These all continue to condition me. Who are they? What do they do? How do they behave? Are they above me or below me on the ladder? (That remains a favourite malpractice.) Are they of use or not? Is the friendship worth it? Do I, after all this time, have even the first glimmerings of compassion in me, or am I deciding by last week's weather forecast?

Everything around me is measured in terms of 'value' and 'usefulness' rather than 'trustfulness'. All this, all the controls that hour by hour, minute by minute, I exercise over myself and society exercises over me, start to be exposed, to be 'seen', in my attempts to stay with the Three Hours.

I open and finish with words. Silence however is fundamental, leading as it does to the apparent fruitlessness of waiting. For Brother Roger of Taizé "prayer is waiting".

I keep returning to a mantra during the hours to help me focus and refocus my vacillating concentration. I am not at all system-atic. I drift. I have no list. For me it seems to be more important to hang around, to be available, to be a space, rather to make it another task to complete. I try to peel off the daily information highway with its endless pile-up of new and secondhand words so as to allow as much emptying as I am able to offer.

Even so I do tour the world a bit. I have particular situations that seem to be given to me to visit and re-visit. I tell myself that I am choosing to wait with those who in this life have no choice but to wait. But I have to admit that this leaves me very much an outsider still, because I can choose to move away, whereas they can't. I choose to give time rather than have it taken from me. And at the end of it all I walk away and have a cup of tea.

Sometimes I fall asleep. Sometimes I am glad. Sometimes I am appalled by my slack, my inattention. Not infrequently I feel defeated, always seeking to turn again into the silence. Monica Furlong writes that "we use every trick, every device open to us to dodge the moment we dread, the moment of 'letting go', of 'yielding'…Yet it is precisely this which silence must achieve."

Is this adoration? I can only trust that, though I feel like a blunt instrument, all that is going on is sharper than a two-edged sword slipping through the place where no created being can hide, where everything is uncovered and open. And I could not *not* keep the Three Hours now unless, as happens occasionally, some other situation has to have absolute priority at that time.

Are there fruits? Well, some thing are sharper and simpler and my priorities seem clearer. I certainly see more directly what unlove is, though this still only just coming into vision. It is a great mystery, and it feels important deliberately to place myself into this mystery – of God in me and throughout all creation – by attempting to allow everything else to be taken away for a while. It is the mystery of the movement from here to there which is caught in the words of this familiar prayer, the noon prayer for peace offered first at the United Nations Disarmament Conference in 1982:

> Lead us from death to life, from falsehood to truth.
> Lead us from despair to hope, from fear to trust.
> Lead us from hate to love, from war to peace.
> Let peace fill our hearts, our world, our universe.

✤

LETTER TWENTY-THREE
All Saints to Advent 1997

This is an ugly letter. But the Three Hours cannot avoid the world's ugliness. Often we try to give it a mark-up with our religious exaggerations until it is almost like asking, Did you have a nice crucifixion?

It is not that I am consumed by the world's ugliness, not at all. But I see ever more clearly – though a slow learner – that joy and gratitude, if they are to be rooted and substantial and not mere froth and bubble, can rise up in the heart only on the further side of the worst.

So I focus on the film *Trainspotting*, the 'film of the decade', as they say. If I had known about it beforehand I might deliberately have missed it. It was not a film, I was told afterwards, for my generation. It is about the very shit of human experience. It is about addiction, in this case, heroin. If the word shit offends, it has to. Perhaps we don't use it enough in our God talk. We dress it up. I could be politely theological or poetic and talk about 'the dross of darkness', but shit says it better. It is what we have to deal with every day, our own and other people's.

The shit is what we are invited to descend into during the Three Hours, to face all the addictions which paralyze and pollute the world, starting with our own. They are the shapes we have been screwed into by our culture, and which we have been content to assume as ours, until they have become second nature: the respectable lazy greeds, the lust to be well thought of, to *be* somebody, the imperceptibly ruthless reshaping of other people to fit our own images and appetites, the comfortable habit of incessant daily gradings and judgments of others, forever separating us from them. "Thank God I am not as other men are." "I wish I were…" The list is endless – the desire to appear good in our work out there or in our hidden prayer – these sickly sweet heroins, these behaviours which are not *hors d'oeuvres* but ordure.

They are the substance of the world's obsessions: approval, power, prestige, success – the four horsemen of our apocalypse.

The first thing I have to do is to recognize that their hold on me is so pervasive that they feel like the real me. I don't even see them. I have to accept that I am an addict and learn to face up to this truth. If I do not, I shall never begin to meet my real self, that meeting that is the beginning of salvation. And it is at the place where the real me begins to be acknowledged that I meet the real Christ. Yes, it is good and important to explore the personality and the alleyways of our behaviour, but we can spend our whole lives searching these mazes and never reach the centre: that this is in the end a nakedly spiritual matter, and, however we practise it, a matter of the discipline of again and again going deeply into prayer.

The Three Hours shows so clearly where we and other people are and where we have to go. It marks us indelibly. It is part of humanity's story, and I find it helpful to recognize it as a common descent. We have to empty ourselves of all those things we hold to be of value, and "naked to follow the naked Christ". We feel inept, we feel strange, we feel a deep longing, hardly perceptible at first, but there, beyond everything that we have so far recognized. As we stay in such prayer we become ever more destitute and useless as all our tricks and deceits and manipulations are relentlessly stripped away, and we can never quite return to the surface, to lives of superficial meaning at the surface of a superficial world.

It is here that I begin to face my real enemies, the poisonous Christ-look-alikes in myself, that desperate hall of mirrors. Yet in facing my little shits, my little hitlers, which I have been given and which I have cultivated, I come to recognize them as friends. For they teach me all that I need to know about the real self that I can be: the purity of truth that is in me and also beyond me. This is pure prayer, poor prayer: they are the same. The Dalai Lama, facing all the wounds inflicted on his people in Tibet says gently, "My enemies are my best friends." Where did I hear that before? "Love your enemies."

It feels harsh and hard as we begin to face these dark truths of our shit. But we will never kill them off. Somewhere in it all we need to encounter and embrace gentleness, the gentleness of Christ. Remember how addicts have to be *weaned* from their addictions. The addict in yourself needs to be met with resilient patience, with a beginning over and over again, with seed after seed of compassion, with the infinite tact of the best kind of 'waiter'. And how we so much prefer to be sick with the person we think we are than to be well with the Christ person we truly are. The greatest enemy of love is impatience.

And straightway what we do for ourselves we do for all. Facing ourselves, we face all humanity. We realize that there is no such thing as private prayer. It is the place of total solidarity where we find we are overwhelmed by the great pile of the world's obsessions and their consequences. But what we have also done is to place ourselves in the torrents of compassion and forgiveness that – as the American Indians say – the Great Spirit is incessantly pouring through the life of humankind. By simply being there and staying there we raise forgiveness into all of human consciousness. It takes faith to do this, for we are unnoticed (but by this stage we are not concerned any more to be noticed). It takes faith not to know, not to grasp, not to understand, to be empty, to wait with no apparent outcome, no movement, no gain.

Yet it is true that vigils of prayer – such vigilance – will bring us to the place where we can feel total sorrow and total joy at the same time. Perhaps this is life's greatest gift. And the warm rising dungs of an ill-prepared stable become the holy of holies.

LETTER TWENTY-FOUR
Pentecost 1998

Everything comes to a dead end. There is no way through. We have found ourselves at the end of yet another cul-de-sac in the maze. It looks as if the deeper we reach into the heart and depth of life's meaning, the more we are plunged into puzzlement and contradiction. We start to learn that to become rich we have to be poor, to succeed we have to fail, to be strong we have to be weak, to be truly alive we have to die. We may have started out with everything looking clear cut with words full of meaning, but we end up at this almost unbearable still point where words have run out, meanings have run out, and we have lost all sense of direction and all power of control. "I have many things to tell you but you cannot bear them now." It is as if there are new words of meaning but that we can hear nothing at all. We reach an impasse. Nothing makes sense in the way it used to. What was once life-giving does so no longer. What we thought was true about ourselves and others and our world appears not to be so. We are not 'there' when we think we are and when we think we are not, 'there' we are.

What we imagine to be faith would make us laugh – if we could laugh. Roger was a computer wizard who lived and breathed the mouse, the keys, the icons on the screen. But he said, "It's as if the screen has gone blank. The whole thing has gone down, and there is nothing, nothing I can do to bring it back."

"Live your bliss," we are told. "Try to live with your whole being what you are for." Well, bliss is ecstasy and ecstasy is a changed state. And if we do discover an occasional bliss, if it is revealed to us (another paradox), and we do seek to follow it, it leads us to deep and desperate places of unbliss where we have to relinquish everything that used to give meaning. "In truth, we are usually very far from bliss – or what we are going through makes us think we are." (Jim Cotter)

The way of bliss is a way of contradiction because it eventually burns out all known words. We conjure with them endlessly, but it is no good, they are of no use any more. They have come to the end of their present purpose for us. Silence starts to be the only medium we dare trust. And in this silence, which we have to keep, we are further confused because, occasionally, new meanings suddenly occur to us (are given to us – another paradox) but which we cannot put together in words because we do not seem to have even an alphabet where we can start. They lodge bewilderingly in the heart of contradiction, we cannot begin to translate them so that they can make rational sense. Rather, they translate us into their meaning without our knowing what is going on. With hidden movement and hidden language, is this what it means to 'live our bliss'?

Laurence Freeman is a Benedictine monk who is the spiritual guide of the World Community for Christian Meditation. Visiting a meditation group in the Washington Correctional Centre for Women (note the irony, WCCM and WCCW!) he was reminded that in prison there is a terrible dehumanising, a stripping away of everything we usually take for granted. Here "there is little of the pretence and pretentiousness that characterize so much of respectable life in the outside world."

In this year of bliss 1998 I find myself meeting all the time those who, living out their bliss with all their heart and soul and mind and strength, have been or have become inmates in prisons of devouring darkness. It feels not too much to say that they have found themselves led, called, into their own personal 'auschwitz' – which is inevitably also the world's – and into the heart of the mystery.

Quasi-mystics like myself talk about self-emptying, choosing the way of silence because it feels as if that is where we are. 'Here's your bliss. Enter it.' Such volunteered discipline has its rightful place, it is perhaps some kind of preparation. It is also universes away from finding yourself being emptied away, being poured out with nothing to replace what has gone. 'To leave all behind and follow' either has totally new meaning or is completely meaningless. You realize that you cannot even think that you can save yourself. Everything has gone. There is no sitting safely on the bank of the river, your 'time of prayer' done, your 'faithful day' completed. The torrent carries you away, roaring and roaring into the immense Silence. These are the inmates, I am but the prison visitor. I leave when I choose.

These lives are characterized by understatement. Perhaps that's another way of describing humility. Whatever they find themselves saying or doing is a complete understatement in relation to the depths at which they are struggling to live, striving to be true. Yet, for me, they are those who are starting to live the world as God lives it, beyond human thought, sense, understanding. They create each moment as it arrives, heaving life out of mere existence, confronting bleakness where it is to be found, and first of all within themselves. This is 'the secret of love, hidden from eternity.'

Here is my freehand of a quotation from Denis Potter (via Jim Cotter): They are experiencing God as present in the quick of their being, in the present tense only, in the fibre and pulse of the minute by minute world. As one of them said, "When I start to pray in words, in meanings, God is not present. When I stop praying, God is."

I owe much in this letter to Jim Cotter's book *Brainsquall*. Without reservation I point you in that direction. He seeks to recount his journey into and through a complete mental breakdown, but for me it is about priesthood. Priesthood is coming to recognize that you are a nobody and a nothing. Priests, lay or ordained, men or women, know that they are nobodies. It is religion that seeks to make them into somebodies – all that glory, laud, and honour. When you start to recognize that you are a nobody and a nothing, you start to live in the world at ease and there is nowhere you go where you do not feel at home. Dag Hammarsjøld, Secretary General of the United Nations in the late fifties and early sixties, wrote in his diary, later published as *Markings*, "Be grateful as your deeds become less and less associated with your name, as your feet ever more lightly tread the earth." Yet he also said, "Long ago, you gripped me, Slinger. *Now* into the storm. *Now* towards your target."

Bliss arrives, it seems, in rare fragments. "Eternity," says R. S. Thomas, "is in the understanding that that little is more than enough." May glimpses come again, in his words once more, to these good companions (as to Moses) of "the miracle of the lit bush".

LETTER TWENTY-FIVE
All Saints to Advent 1998

Between All Saints at the beginning of November and Advent at its end we experience the procession of days down into the darkest time of the year. It has just gone eleven on the eleventh day of the eleventh month. People are called to be silent and remember: to remember the wounds of war and the desolations of our continuing inhumanity. It has been suggested that the twentieth century will be remembered as the Century of the Holocaust ...the dark burning, the stench of roasted life, of sickly rot. And wars remain. And Auschwitz returns again and again to haunt us. We keep two minutes' silence 'lest we forget'. And we do, very readily, thank you very much.

We need to be reminded that we are caught up in the mystery of a corporate evil for which we are in part always responsible. We are co-destroyers as well as victims. We are killers as well as saviours. This person's death by cancer, that person's savage mental collapse: they are intricately traceable to me, they are part of the world I make, part of me. I cannot help it. I am helplessly responsible.

The Three Hours stands in human history to remind us of all this, and at the same time to show us the way through. As Laurence Freeman puts it, "The wounds of Christ's death could be healed only when he immersed himself in the dark depths of his divinity." The Three Hours is to be entered into in order to make us ever more open to the dark depths in which we are immersed, and to reveal that at the heart of this abyss is not guilt nor self-flagellation, not blankness nor the emptiness of despair, but our own divinity. It is given to us that we may embrace all things. Indeed, without gathering the chaos of holocaust into our arms, we cannot grow into the fulness of the divine life which awaits us, at every moment, and in so doing we run the risk of rendering futile much else of what we do.

What an irony that the Sunderland Football Club has named its new park the Stadium of Light! What a delicious irony that the government has not been able to find commercial backing to finance the Spirit place in the Millennium Dome. Of course not! We live in an age of profound darkness when all definitions of God have become eclipsed. We become ever more sharply aware that the world's religions will never themselves satisfy, only point a way. In order to proclaim God we have to live part of our life of prayer willing to be led down the steeps of darkness into the abyss. We are like the Tommy of the First World War, shit scared of going over the top and into the unknown. We are like the multitude of Jews herded through the gates to see in front of them the smoking sacrifice billowing out of the chimney.

Am I being melodramatic? Well, I believe we embrace something real when we descend to the places where prayers are groans which lie too deep for words. Just as it is necessary that the world observes Remembrance, so it is necessary, as those young men and women did, to stand in silence time and time again facing the gas ovens that still burn so brightly in the human heart. As Alan Ecclestone put it, "Much prayer has wilted and died for lack of silence to enable it to be prayer at all." The Three Hours is part of our inheritance, and we are called to claim *all* that has been given to us.

Close to home, in the desolation of Omagh, the nation was reminded of the evil in which we are all entangled. We stopped

and gawped with silent bewildered faces. People knew then that
to use words would only diminish the horror. So we must learn
from their standing silences, their awkwardness. But we also
need to volunteer such 'gawpings' at other freer times, not
simply in response to the bad things that hit us. It is of course
paltry, useless prayer, for which we shall always feel unprepared.
Yet it is also somehow the best that we can at that moment give
– like flowers laid on wet pavements. Such weakness, such fragil-
ity, even at its bleakest, is a sort of redemption. At the very least
it is a determination, no matter what, to begin again, to live,
again and again, our dark divinity. It was the way T. S. Eliot
pointed to: "Let the darkness come upon you which shall be the
darkness of God."

To contemplate the sheer scale of the Holocaust, the extremes
of human degradation that seep into the fabric of our lives,
demanding our attention day by day, is to be bemused, hypno-
tized, paralyzed. Yet there is a greater vastness, that of the Mercy
which is the breathing membrane of all creation. It is this that the
Three Hours enables us to enter: it opens us to "the scale of the
power of mercy", in words of Rowan Williams. Jesus 'hangs' in
wordless prayer in his own being, drawing the evil into the mercy,
and he beckons us to do the same. We are called to let ourselves
sink deep into the roots of our own evil, and there to be set free
to decontaminate one another, the Church, and the world. Of
course we would rather do anything than be so helpless, so sur-
rendered. But at this crossroads of undoing, unmaking, and
remaking, as in all prayer, "it is not I who look, but I who am
looked through." (R. S. Thomas)

Then comes the Holy Babe! Into the darkest time of the year
comes the 'Saviour', a word we address to a pink and puking
scrap of humanity, slithering like each one of us, helpless into the
world. As Augustine said, he comes penetrating our deafness with
his loud crying. It is a riddle: How can he be a saviour unless we
come to rescue him from the perils of being born?

Here, once again, is Etty, who volunteered to enter the
concentration camp with her fellow Jews, speaking with praise

and promise for us all, words that can somehow redeem any Auschwitz and forestall any others.

> I shall try to help you, God, to stop my strength ebbing away, though I cannot vouch for it in advance. But one thing is becoming increasingly clear to me: that you cannot help us, that we must help you to help ourselves. And that is all that we can manage these days, and also all that really matters: that we safeguard that little piece of you, God, in ourselves. And perhaps in others as well. Alas, there doesn't seem to be much you yourself can do about our circumstances, about our lives. Neither do I hold you responsible. You cannot help us, but we must help you and defend your dwelling place inside us to the last.

LETTER TWENTY-SIX
All Saintstide 1999

This is my only letter this year. An exhibition on Tyneside, concerned with genocide, landscape, and memory, showed the visitor a series of photographs of sites where atrocities have taken place. It was called *For most of it I have no words*.

That is how it has been for me. And that is how it so often is for so many people. The events in Kosovo took my guts away, humanity's deadly flourish of a signature to sign off the twentieth century of holocausts. Then there is the Best of British, we who have underwritten the terrors which have raged in East Timor through our highly successful arms trade with the Indonesian government. Stretching the memory back to the beginning of the century, I recall, with the help of a recent television programme, 'the novelty' of concentration camps set up by the British for Boer families and black Africans during the Boer War.

Frances Wilkinson writes with a clean fire and a bright hand in her late eighties. She is part of the jet stream of spirituality which burns, which burnishes the Church at its heart and cheers me on. She writes to remind us that we are all implicated in these wider events, not least Balfour's promise of a homeland to the Zionists in return for money for armaments, and the consequent conflicts between two peoples struggling for land and identity which we all take with us into the next century, seemingly as far from resolution as ever.

I like her use of the word 'implicated' because she goes on to say that the amazing thing about the life of Jesus was that he was *not* implicated. The word penetrates the pap that is so often the regular church diet, those words handed out like analgesics Sunday by Sunday in language worn too smooth. To refer to Jesus in this way makes some sense of his being 'without sin'. He had nothing to hide. No wonder he didn't last long.

In the end of course all words become pap. At their best they grow out of silence and lead back into silence, but we go on blabbering long after we should stop. This is why coming home to silence is a fundamental necessity in the rhythm of our lives.

One or two of you have written to say, Cheer up, it's not all that bad. Why go on so much about darkness? Jesus is Light, the Light of the world. And yes, I do continue to be amazed and grateful that hope persistently bubbles up inside me. But it is so clear to me that that light can be glimpsed only at the end of the tunnel and that the light perceived before darkness is superficial. It is, however, where many people dwell.

So this letter, written at All Saintstide (it is my favourite 'tide', the one on whose swell I rode into the Church), simply sets down my indebtedness and my thankfulness to all the saints, to the Solidarity, who through my lifetime have kept me on track with their words, their presences, and their silences. They have encouraged me to stay deep and allow myself to go deeper, turning my face again and again towards the unfaceable. They give me courage to "endure spiritual weather without dismay", as Alan Ecclestone put it, to keep on keeping on.

Here a few names, with their words, but there are so many others, nameless ones who have felt themselves required – or have simply been driven — to work underground, in the dark, with everything a blank, and to do so with courage and endurance. I say to them, The light in the middle of your head occasionally winks to me in the dark distances, somewhere ahead of me. Always, somehow, there is someone just around the next bend, sturdily fumbling along an unknown way.

But here are the words of a few of the others. I string them together in a kind of celebration of Presence.

Because the Three Hours would not organize itself for me to fit into painlessly, I decided a few weeks ago to abandon it. Silly really. As if one can choose to abandon the Presence that overwhelms, even *in absentia*. So I've given up abandoning. I'm going back to the un-home that is the nearest thing I know to home on earth.

What I find really hard about the Three Hours is precisely that it opens a place for pain to pour haemorrhaging into consciousness. I've been unable to make that awareness fit comfortably with my sense of the vitality of things, my faith in the resurrection. I find myself oscillating, plummeting, from one pole to another: life seems wonderful, life seems hopeless. Although I know well enough that this is not a rehearsal but the real thing, I still feel that a real peace-builder would have these poles relate easily within himself.

DOUG CONSTABLE

Nevertheless the darkness and silence appal. The darkness and the light are both alike to God, in the realm of darkness his wonders are known, but human beings are not God, and but for his help we could not endure it. Those Jews and non-Jews who in the dark years took their lives were no cowards but men and women whom the darkness destroyed. It was not the unthinking or shallow who measured the horror but those who in fineness of spirit were overwhelmed.

This night sky of the Lord that has become the condition of our time and has been experienced in the anguish of the death camps and the bewilderment of sufferers round the world is still, so faith affirms, the darkness where God is.

ALAN ECCLESTONE
The Night Sky of the Lord

Only to the extent that man exposes himself over and over again to annihilation can that which is indestructible arise within him. In this lies the dignity of daring. Thus the aim of practice is not to develop an attitude which allows a man to acquire a state of harmony and peace wherein nothing can ever trouble him. On the contrary, practice should teach him to let himself be assaulted, perturbed, moved, insulted, broken, battered, that is to say, it should enable him to dare to let go of his futile hankering after harmony, surcease from pain, and a comfortable life, in order that he may discover, in doing battle with the forces that oppose him, that which awaits him beyond the world of opposites. The first necessity is that we should have courage to face life and to encounter all that is perilous in the world. When this is possible, meditation becomes the means by which we accept and welcome the demons which arise from the unconscious, a process very different from the practice of concentration on some object as a protection against such forces. Only if we venture repeatedly through zones of annihilation can our contact with Divine Being, which is beyond annihilation, become firm and stable. The more a man learns wholeheartedly to confront the world that threatens him with isolation, the more are the depths of the Ground of Being revealed and the possibilities of new life and becoming opened.

AUTHOR UNKNOWN
sent to me by Samara Joldersma

What the Church will need as its priests is men and women who know that the important and obvious thing about God is that he is silent. He does not speak. He does not grunt, or shuffle his feet, or cough, or do anything to assure us he is there. He meets us in his silence. The last words of Jesus in St Mark's Gospel are, "My God, my God, why have you forsaken me?" He has been given nothing to say. It had all been given to Pilate, the soldiers, the chief priests, the scribes, the passers-by, and the centurion; they said who he was, mocking him, in unbelief. He was silent, and Pilate was amazed, God was silent, and Jesus was desolate. This is the way.

What the Church needs is people who believe in shutting up; that God is not a talking God, that we do not have the word of God, we have the silence of God. That's all there is, and that's what makes us tick; that's what we want to bring others into.

JOHN FENTON

LETTER TWENTY-SEVEN
All Saintstide 2000

Simone Weil, one of the twentieth century's most penetrating mystics, said of prayer, "One does not seek God. One waits for God." Patience, hesitation, waiting: these are her watchwords for prayer. I would want to extend that to 'One waits *with* God,' since waiting *for* suggests a God out there, apart from. Sixty years on from her writing we are growing into a realization that God is utterly and always present.

Laurence Freeman, the spiritual guide of the World Community for Christian Meditation, talks of our being in a new age of Presence. This is why so much of our prayer and liturgy do not captivate, seem outworn to the many who are seeking, because they carry the language of distance and explanation, not nearness and mystery. The old language is that of plea-bargaining, of trying to attract God's attention, to get God to call on us. We might be waiting, yes, but it is like standing on a station platform looking at the arrivals board and wondering if God will be on the next train. This does not resonate at all with people's confused experience of spiritual encounter in the twentieth-first century. 'Presence' is indeed a better name for God.

Prayer is waiting: simply that, nothing more. That simplicity costs not less than everything, as Dietrich Bonhoeffer realized. I recently read a thesis by David Peel which is called *Ordinary Glory*, supported by the Cedarwood Trust. It is the result of twenty years' work in one of the most deprived and despised communities in the country: Meadow Well in North Shields, one of those places that has suffered riots. He writes of twenty years of waiting, of hanging around not *for* these broken people, humiliated by decades of deprivation, but *with* them, sharing the minutest detail of their often mutilated outer and inner lives, besieged by unemployment, poverty, criminality, and rejection. It is a waiting with them, trusting the good heart in them, the Presence within them, to emerge in glimmers, in small fitful gestures, and sometimes into full day, at their right time. This is not the police's time, not the courts' time, not a hurrying world's time, not a let's see the results now time, but their right time. It is to wait *with* the God in them.

This is not exactly to wait in darkness, for waiting *is* darkness, impenetrable, opaque, obscure, because the God who is with us and everywhere present, is concealed. "God," said Meister Eckhart, all those centuries ago, "is closer to us than we are to ourselves." And you can't get more concealed than that. In prayer, God *is* darkness, and it requires infinite patience, renewed day by day, even to begin to 'know' the Presence, to become aware of how the Presence makes itself uniquely present to each one of us. Each encounter with the eternal compassion is unique. There is also something of hesitation about it, that tact which is characteristic of all true love, a determination not to crush or confine us, however limited our freedom may seem to be. "A smouldering wick he will not quench." It is a kind of shadow dancing, this being with God. As T. S. Eliot put it, "So the darkness shall be light and the stillness the dancing." The Hindus have a lovely word for it: 'Advaita', not one and not two, which is the core meaning of unity.

So we are moving into an age of 'knowing', of recognizing and accepting that we are held in Mystery. As Tom Joldersma described it from a physicist's perspective, we are bound into the "irreducible complexity of things".

How much we all need the patience, the slowness. We need to recapture it in the life of the Church, instead of rushing to fill every space because it is empty and dark and unknown. It is better to hesitate, to rest, to let oneself enter the dark waiting, to tremble at the threshold of another's life, to start to know even as I am known.

God is so close that God is utterly different, closer than anything we can describe as close. We have no words to describe this closeness. The word 'close' is as near as we can get. God is "so different that that difference is different from all the differences we can think of. God is not different from me as I am different from you. God is different from that kind of difference." (from a conference address by Rowan Williams) All we can say is that we need to draw closer and closer and begin to 'know' the ultimate mystery in all its difference.

Rather than rooting around looking for meanings we need to live the meaning without trying to give it words. We need to accept the darkness, to live the darkness, to let the Mystery that is darkness unfold in us, to become bearers of that Mystery. This is the work of faith – and faith is dark. We have to stop the vain scrabbling attempts to show the world that we have the answers. All that we have are the questions. We are the bearers of the questions.

Waiting does not mean doing nothing. David Peel and his response to Meadow Well shows that. The waiting which is darkness starts to cut through all the demands for action which confront us until we are able to recognize 'the one thing necessary' for us to be engaged in, and to leave the rest. Leaving the rest is often the hardest part because we don't want to think we are missing anything! We want to leave our options open in case we have made the wrong decision. We want to be well thought of, to get in on this and that act. But we have to recognize our own narrow gate and go through it. For we are all mystics now, embedded in the Mystery as much as in primeval slime from both of which we come. And we have to act accordingly. Thomas

Moore in *Original Self* puts it like this: "We have to allow the soul to take over and from a dimmer place take the lead."

The world desperately needs communities of people who are on the move, not here, there, and everywhere, spiritually touring around, but deliberately moving to a deeper place, people who move with patient confidence, unafraid of space and the dark, unafraid of the passing away, the emptying of things, unafraid of transcendence, people who, because they wait, find themselves being held and honoured and transfigured in the beauty of a greater and greater love at the heart of life.

Eric Abbott conducted the Three Hours service in Lincoln Cathedral on Good Friday in 1944. He was looking for people who "after long paddling in the shallows, dare one day to jump in at the deep end, and find that they can swim." (By the way, he also suggested that the Three Hours should be spent in silence.)

Without waiting nothing can happen. Without the pause there is no music.

> ...I had to relinquish all the powers I normally command. I had to relinquish, above all, the sense and affect of *activity*. I had to allow – and this seemed horrible – the sense and feeling of *passivity*. I found this humiliating at first, a mortification of my self, the active, masculine, ordering self which I had equated with my science, my self-respect, my mind. And then, mysteriously, I began to change, to allow, to welcome this abdication of activity. I began to perceive this change on the third day of limbo. To the soul, lost, confounded in the darkness, the long night, neither charts, nor the chart-making mind, were of service. These active qualities might be valuable later, but at this point they had nothing to work on. For my state in the dark night was one of passivity, an intense and absolute and essential passivity, in which action – any action – would be useless and a distraction. The watchwords at this time were, "Be patient...endure...wait...be still...do nothing...don't think!" How difficult, how paradoxical, a lesson to learn!
>
> OLIVER SACKS
> *A Leg to Stand on*

Both the Old and the New Testaments describe our existence in relation to God as one of waiting. The condition of our relation to God is first of all one of *not* having, *not* seeing, *not* knowing, and *not* grasping. A religion in which that is forgotten, no matter how ecstatic or active or reasonable, replaces God by its own creation of an image of God. I am convinced that much of the rebellion against Christianity is due to the overt or veiled claim of the Christians to possess God, and therefore, also, to the loss of this element of waiting, so decisive for the prophets and the apostles. They did not possess God; they waited for him. For how can God be possessed? Is God a thing that can be grasped and known among other things? Is God less than a human person? Since God is infinitely hidden, free, and incalculable, we must wait for him in the most absolute and radical way. He is God for us just in so far as we do *not* possess him. We are stronger when we wait than when we possess. When we possess God, we reduce God to that small thing we knew and grasped of God; and we make it an idol.

PAUL TILLICH, from 'Waiting'
The Shaking of the Foundations

It would be unnecessary as well as an impossible undertaking here to review the testimony of the great mystics of the ages. They have found their way while living into such an assurance of union and communion with God that for them there is nothing they can apprehend that death can do to endanger this community of spirit with Spirit. The greatest of them have made the discovery that there is an unlost soul-centre in the deeps of our being which has never 'gone out' from God. There is a *synteresis*, or central substance – the very self of our self, as Meister Eckhart would say – which belongs in common with God and with us. As the unborn child is attached at a certain point to the mother, the mark of which remains for ever afterwards, so, although no physical parallel can truly imagine it, this inmost soul-centre binds us back indissolubly into the life of our spiritual Origin, and like a tugging natal cord of life connects us with our Source.

For the mystic this Something of God in us is not a theory or speculation, but a first-hand apprehension which makes Eternal Life into the one real life, and the transitory, temporal stage a parable…of the real life in God.

RUFUS M. JONES
The Radiant Life

LETTER TWENTY-EIGHT
All Saintstide 2001

Perhaps our Creed should begin, "We believe in the absence of God," for it would acknowledge that there is no way we can see a visible Presence. We receive only hints and intimations, and these of the barest kind. Most contemporary Christian religious practice still struggles to get God 'into the frame'. We try to bring God into close-up, so that focusing on one set of images or another we can say, "Thar she blows!" (or, more meanly, "There, I told you so,") to a world struggling yet not able to believe. Yet the God we love, the energy which both calls us and drives us, is always just out of the picture, the shape that casts a shadow at the edge which you can barely discern. I find much more sympathy with the person who cried out as the Twin Towers fell, "I prayed and prayed. I didn't know what words to use. There is NO GOD." I am nearer that person than the one who said, "I know where my God was that morning. He was very busy. First of all, he was trying to discourage anyone from taking this flight: those four flights could together have held a thousand people and there were only 266 aboard. He was busy trying to create obstacles for employees at the World Trade Centre: after all, only around 20,000 were at the towers when the first jet hit. He was holding up two buildings, each a hundred and ten storeys, so that two-thirds of the workers could get out."

That is for me so far from truth. It is that old worn-out God who makes judgments quite arbitrarily about who shall live and who shall die on a bright, sunlit, terrible morning. Once we take a fix on God, there is no God. God is absent in any way we are used to making God present. This is what we have to grow up into in these our times. There is a fine and vigorous morality – equality, recognition of sexual minorities, human rights, one world, hospice care, etc – growing up without belief in God. Rhetoric about Christian values – even worse, Christian family values – gets us nowhere. To gain a glimmer of the love of God, of the Energy of creation, we have to get beyond this thinking. Rowan Williams writes, "Whatever Jesus makes possible must be more than spectacular improvements to the human condition." We have to be prepared, even to volunteer, to enter the darkness, the mystery of creation, and wait in deep silence, to lose every picture and holy concept we may have, and wait to be surprised, to be horrified, overwhelmed, blown *out of* our minds. Come, Holy Spirit, come.

To embrace the dark does not mean we have no hope. But it does mean we have to abandon the optimism which envisages the neat happy endings we would like. The Chief Rabbi, Jonathan Sacks, has written in a recent edition of *The Tablet*:

> Optimism is the belief that things are going to get better, hope is the belief that together we can make them better. So I believe that hope is precisely what we, as religious leaders, have to offer the world by joining together to make thing better.

We have to look into the waste places and inhabit them as much as we can. It is a dimension of prayer that is urgently needed, even fundamental to the renewal we all long for. So much of what we have inherited in our religious traditions has shrunk, and so much in our materialist culture has shrivelled the human spirit. Even the Twin Towers, with all the achievements they represented, were also symbols of greed and pride and unbounded egotism.

We have to contemplate that collapse, gaze vainly into the cracks and twists, wait at the places where everything has split

apart and we can make no connections, the points of contradiction which seem to exclude any possibility of Presence. We have
to inhabit the impossible, unbelievable place. We have to journey
to the dead end from which only the truth of life will come.

Perhaps the only place where we can begin to 'see' as we look
back on that fearful morning is the 343 firemen and rescue
workers crushed and broken, and the priest administering the last
rites himself killed by another falling body – and the mobile
phone messages, "I love you," and "I'm not going to get out of
this." In the desolate, dark land of an absent God there appeared
these glimmers of light where people were doing what they felt
they had to do, regardless of consequence. It all seems waste and
futility, all those brave acts. There is nowhere to look except at
'the foolishness of God'. Or, with Jacob, "Truly God is in this
place and I did not know it." All we have to go on are those
moments of sheer compassion, of selfless acts carried out in fear
and trembling with unrestrained courage, in the utter darkness of
all crucifixions. We may come to see them as divining moments.

New York, they say, has been quiet since the disaster, slower,
more reflective as well as fearful. For Laurence Freeman, "In a
moment of transcendence there are no trivial pursuits." Are we
humans beginning to grow up in the midst of this darkness?
St Mark describes Jesus as going out to pray in the darkness well
before dawn. That is our prayer too now, to be persistent, steady,
silent, watching and waiting. We are bidden to look and listen and
not be afraid, to launch out into the deep.

We are being caught up into the whole wasteful dynamic of
creation, the sheer extravagance of living and dying. Every
human life is caught up in the heart of this, however unaware we
may be. We cannot isolate ourselves from the rest of creation by
keeping company with a domesticated God who must be on our
side and against all the others.

We would like to know where we fit in. But we are so small. We
are aware of ourselves only as a single frame in a long film about
which we know nothing. Annie Dillard calculates that "the
average size of all living animals, including man, is almost that

of a house fly." She sees the Creator working with "a spendthrift genius and an extravagance of care," and wonders if God has the same affectionate disregard for human life as for the rest of creation. This God we cannot know, we can only wait for.

Nearly always, it seems, God's 'appearing' is in sudden moments of upheaval and confusion, strange violence, bewildering compassion, troubled darkness, disturbing awe. My list begins with Abraham, Jeremiah, Ezekiel, the transfiguration of Jesus, Paul: you can make your own – it is endless.

Francis Dewar reminds us that "God's primary calling to us is…to spend time in his presence…Prayer is totally useless and utterly important." Prayer, says, Rowan Williams, is "obstinate uselessness". We can begin to see truly only if we practise letting go of what we think we see. When we become our prayer in this way, if we 'be it' rather than 'do it' we start to live more and more in the present moment, and it is only there that we have any hope of living the Mystery. Buddhists forcefully remind Christians that constant daily mindfulness (which some of them call 'Holy Spirit') is the only way of cancelling out our otherwise constant tendency to forgetfulness. Without daily mindfulness the press of contemporary events keeps swamping us out of reality into the pre-packaged solutions everywhere on offer.

The dark waiting of the person who becomes a prayer is often experienced as quite useless, a sheer waste of time, so empty that it identifies exactly with those waste places where we might be transfixed by a glimpse of God's appearing. It is at such places, at such moments, that we may discover that rather than gazing we are being gazed upon. "I had been all my life a bell and never knew it until that moment I was lifted and struck. The vision comes and goes, mostly goes, but I live for it." (Annie Dillard, *Pilgrim at Tinker Creek*)

These days, after many years of praying little or not at all, I get up shortly after 6.15 in the morning. I make a mug of tea and, clasping it to me like a comforter, I sit cross-legged on the floor in my living room, in front of a Rublev ikon of the Trinity and a candle. I have a big hourglass and I tip it upside down and abandon the hour to God. This is waste of time prayer, holocaust time. I often feel really lousy, tired, nauseated, dreadful, and I long to creep back to bed, but I do not because this is God's time, not mine, and I know that its quality lies not in what I feel but in the totality of my gift. This is a time of abandonment to God, a time in which I try to still my mind and just be open, receptive to him. My prayer is totally without images and largely without words... After twenty years, this emptying of the mind comes relatively easily to me, or perhaps it is more accurate to say that I am more relaxed about it than I used to be. If, as usually happens, my mind is invaded by a kaleidoscope of thoughts and ideas I simply ignore them...Some thoughts of course are too insistent to be ignored, and so I gather them up and include them in my prayer.

SHEILA CASSIDY

Young
I pronounce you. Older
I still do, but seldomer
now, leaning far out
over an immense depth, letting
your name go and waiting,
somewhere between faith and doubt,
for the echoes of its arrival.

R. S. THOMAS

This is the place of prayer.
Here, where the inward-pointing nails
converge.
The ever-narrowing gate
intersection
when the world of time and space
yields up its measured form.

Here in the needle's eye
dark upon dark.
The aching, echoing void
of the hollowed heart
suspended
at the point of change.

Unknowing
(and that is the agony)
bearing the unknown
to the mystery
at the place of prayer.

MAY CROWTHER
quoted in Jim Cotter, *Prayer at Night*

LETTER TWENTY-NINE
All Saintstide 2002

Whatever became of innocence? It seems such a distant word these days, merely the echo of a dream. Of course we still revel momentarily in childhood innocence when it appears around us: the wide-eyed 'nowness' of the very young, their gift of living utterly in the moment and seeing miracles every day, everywhere, the immediate brightness following tears, their totally open commentary on life ("Mummy you've painted your hair" – she'd had it dyed), their suddenly beginning to skip for no better reason than simply being alive, the singing and laughing that shakes the bones. It all seems such a long time ago.

Of course we lose this sense of innocence early enough, when we sense we are being betrayed: the love we looked for and took for granted until it never came, the promise broken – perhaps for the best of reasons, the compromises we were offered, sometimes cheap bids for our loyalty and affection, short cuts to loving which we swallowed open mouthed. There were the injustices when our word was not heard, the impatience and the anger that flowed above our heads that we did not understand, though they often left us with the sense that we were to blame.

So we learned in our own turn to do unto others, to enter ourselves into the clever games of betraying and selling short until it comes to feel like a true part of ourselves, second nature, as we get lost in a forest of a thousand compromises, experts in glib side-stepping and world weariness.

Words such as innocence and purity seem lost for ever in a guilty and dirty world. We spin around, disorientated by confusion and half-truths and uncertainties. People may be wide-eyed, but not in wonder, rather in anxiety and fear. Nothing can now escape the brooding eye of instant, universal, personal, and corporate communication, and as lies are exposed by counter lies trust becomes a rare commodity.

Is it possible to see this world laid bare as the prelude to greater things? To be able to see through all the duplicities, bombarded by doubts and uncertainties may be a gain, providing us with a new starting point. It does not feel that way, but it may be so.

In the Three Hours of the dying of Jesus we may find a guide into and through our present world darkness, for they tell us that innocence and purity are not lost, only covered over, and that they can be restored. Betrayal and crucifixion are innocence despoiled, but by choosing to be there, to stand there, to embrace the darkness, to wait silently, choosing nothing else, the recovery of innocence is at hand.

St John of the Cross put it like this: "To awaken to the great heart of Jesus we must be willing to tread for a long time as a blind man in the darkness." We have only to accept the invitation to descend into the darkness, into the abyss of love's mystery, to stay there with the helplessness of watching and waiting, to be immovable in our trust in the goodness of life when so much seems to erode it. We have to stay there, saying No to all that assails us, all that is less than love, all that comes to us in holy as well as unholy disguises, and saying Yes when the suffering is so immense that hope is no longer hope as we used to know it, and panic hits us. We have to go through the distress, quietly and persistently, and rest in the faith that nothing can separate us from the love of God, whatever that means and whenever it is impossible to understand what it means.

It is a place we have to return to again and again, to stay there in prayer when it feels utterly beyond our strength, when bones ache with the absence of any sense of what it means to pray, when everything is hollowed out and eyes are blank with looking: to stay, to watch, to wait, as if it is utterly pointless, and to say, Yet I will.

This is the groaning and travailing that Paul hints at in Romans 8. We have to endure despair and not turn aside. We are called to embrace it, to surrender to it, for the sake of the world. Someone has to 'be there' and at the same time to insist that there is more to it than this worst, to hold on to the conviction that there is a beyond that is nowhere in sight, to call it into being by our presence and to be able to recognize the gift of its appearing when it happens. Such surrender leads us towards the recovery of innocence and purity, and to recognize its beauty.

Francis Dewar reminds us that Thomas Merton talks of a virgin point just before dawn.

> The first chirps of the waking day birds mark the 'point vierge' of the dawn under a sky as yet without real light, a moment of awe and inexpressible innocence, when the Father in perfect silence opens their eyes. They begin to speak to him, not with fluent song but with an awakening questioning that is their dawn state, their state at the 'point vierge'. Their condition asks if it is time for them to 'be'. He answers Yes. Then, one by one, they wake up and become birds. They manifest themselves as birds, beginning to sing. Presently they will be fully themselves, and will even fly. All wisdom seeks to collect and manifest itself at that blind sweet point...the virgin point between darkness and light, between non-being and being.

It is that point we wait for, that point we come to. We do not know what we bring to others but we do know that we bring it. Then we too find ourselves starting to say with Walt Whitman, "As for me I know nothing else but miracles." Bede Griffiths says that the silent prayer of one person transforms the world.

Listen to this boy and his mother, recounted by Wanda Nash in *A Fable for our Time*:

> When the rapist broke into the house he accosted a small boy before attacking his white mother. The young eight year old stood up to him and said, "Go on, do what you like, you can't hurt me because God is here. He is with me, and he is stronger than you." Two years later, in the face of the horrific aftermath of this nightmare, the mother said, "I am still living on the power of that moment. God was with us in that room, and it is the knowledge of that Presence that has held me up through all the terrible consequences that followed. It has never left me."

When evil is borne, it is defeated. To bring a wide-awake fully conscious innocence into our distraught world, to make a way for Presence, is our gift. 'Rays of darkness' are what Rowan Williams calls these mysteries, recalling Dionysius the Areopagite. Without darkness there is no true light. Without embracing the darkness, all other light is false light. The only real light comes through the reflected love of such willing surrender. It is what made the beginning out of darkness.

> The only news I know
> Is bulletins all day
> From immortality.
>
> The only shows I see
> Tomorrow and today,
> Perchance eternity.
>
> The only one I meet
> Is God, the only street
> Existence, this traversed.

If other news there be,
Or admirabler show
I'll tell it you.

EMILY DICKINSON

The way not to drown
Is to swim far out
And dive deep down.

ANONYMOUS

Our whole business in this life is to restore to health
the eye of the heart whereby God may be seen.

AUGUSTINE OF HIPPO

LETTER THIRTY
Pentecost 2003

Darkness. Darkness. Darkness is older than Light. It is there before
the earth was made. "Darkness is no darkness to thee. To thee
the Night is as clear as the Day. To thee Darkness and Light are
both alike." (Psalm 139) And that is true of my own individual
darkness, before and in which I was "fearfully and wonderfully
made", when "I was formed in secret and woven in the depths."

Darkness is the seedbed of creation. True Light does not
replace darkness, it grows out of it and is nourished by it. The
roses now on my summer tree are nourished by the dark earth in
its humble pot.

The Church is descending into darkness. It is darkness that we
need, and darkness is being given to us. The good ship Lollipop
is going down with the rest of the convoy as the established world
order sinks rapidly before our eyes into such depths of confusion

that we cannot predict the outcome. It has to be so. It is necessary and right. It is the way of things. We need to *know* the chaos, the lack of direction, the bewilderment, which being enveloped in total darkness brings. Only so can new creation, true creation, be made where we can rest only on our sense of helplessness. I cannot do anything about it, except being me, here, now. The Church needs this slow fumbling time of darkness.

Rowan Williams has put it slightly differently. He says that one of the first things the Church needs is space, space out of which true hope can grow, but not without clearing the clutter. And this may mean all our present forms of church life, all religious and spiritual luggage.

For such a weary long time we have thought of ourselves as bright and clear as the noonday with no shadow. Perhaps we have allowed it briefly, once a year in Holy Week. Otherwise we have stuck grimly to being triumphant with the one emerging world-conqueror and hero, the spectacular Christ. All else, all other faith systems, all other pictures, all are supposed to fall away and know their place in submission to this victorious Christ. Such certainties have long gone, but so many of us are not yet ready to recognize that their absence is a gift. We still can't quite believe that it is meaningless to dodge to and fro, trying to keep in some kind of spiritual limelight.

We must learn to welcome the darkness of a time when all the lights are going out. All the spurious pictures we have of ourselves and of the things we have made in our own image are challenged and found to be empty. Everything that we thought we were, and who we might or not become, it all has to go. Darkness brings pain, the pain of fear, and it is so hard to learn that this is what we have been feeling all along but we have not really been aware of it. For we have been living in a false daylight, hiding in our puffed up certainties, thinking that we were right, ignoring the hints and suggestions that all might not be as well as we pretended.

There was a woman who lived at the heart of a forest who was supposed to have the secret of Truth, but she was surrounded by mystery and supposed to be fierce. Few who visited her ever returned. Three young men set out to find her. The first came across her stirring a great pot over a blazing fire. "Why have you come?" she asked. "Oh," he said, "they sent me." "Hm," she murmured, and without more ado grabbed hold of him and tossed him into the pot and kept on stirring. The second arrived. "Why have you come?" she asked. "I thought it was something I ought to do," he replied. "Hm," she murmured, and she thrust him into the pot as well. The third young man arrived at the same clearing. "Why have you come?" said the woman once more. He hesitated, and then said, "I don't know." She stopped stirring, smiled and said, "Well then, come into my cottage and live with me."

The interior life is dense and dark. It has always been so. Yet that is where we must find a place to rest, the place where we had life before we knew we were made. It is when we discover ourselves naked, uncovered, defenceless, that the real person emerges, the faithful one, who trusts come what may, who begins to recognize the darkness in others, and far from being alone starts to learn that this is the place where so much in us and all creation always dwells. Darkness becomes palpable and friendly, a place where we can reach out, touch and be touched, where the trust grows without which there is no survival.

It is impossible to run fast, to pant breathless, to keep sunnily cheerful, in the darkness. We have to go gently, quietly, attentive to the slightest sound or tremor, being still, giving our full attention, watching and waiting, alert. Slow footstep by slow footstep we start to distinguish between real pain and false pain, real joy and false joy, discovering how close they lie together.

'Light prayer', with its words, symbols, arguments, images, discriminations (good and bad), and reasonings, is necessary to show us the way to the dark place. 'Dark prayer' is unlike any prayer we have known before. If we are to be made new, it is bound to be a place of nothing, blank, without word or picture or idea. Of course we take such clutter with us, and at first it has to rise to the surface out of the unsettled and frightened corners of our being. They are gifts in so far as we welcome them as part of what we have to let go of if we are to grow in trust.

'Dark prayer' is neither presence nor absence. It contradicts everything we think we know. Where am I? I do not know if I am in the right place, I can but trust that I am. And without realizing we have reached it we come to a place where we tumble and fall into an endless still point. It is the place where the power of creation, the whole energy of Being, begins again and again and forever again. It is, to paraphrase T. S. Eliot, to keep coming back to the beginning, and to know it for the first time. We sense that power of creation by which we are constantly being formed and which is not of our making. We consent to it by our acceptance of darkness, by our descent through our restlessness into waiting, where at some long last perhaps we may be able to recognize for an instant that "there is no doer but God", as Julian of Norwich put it. God is touched for a whole bewildering moment, the length of a heartbeat, at the heart of our own heart, little enough, yet enough.

It is a flash of dazzle, not light. It is dark dazzle. For God's Light is not light in any way we can describe or in the usual ways we experience it. God's Light is utterly elsewhere, and we can see God only darkly. The moments when we know it, always fleeting, come and go, with their gentleness, their exhilaration, their wildness, sometimes contradictory, sometimes grievous. Once in a while it seems that we recognize everything that is. They cannot be sought, they are gifts: it is a mystery, the mystery of unfathomable compassion and limitless hope.

Such darkness is a necessary grace. It is the grace of unknowing. It is the grace that the whole Church has to allow instead of keeping it at arms' length, all the energy going into the stretching and exhausting everyone with the effort. We have to let go and fall into the darkness.

Dark prayer is also an act of profound generosity, a gift that seems to be so wasteful, for it is a giving away of everything. The Church is challenged to do exactly that. It is the apparent waste and generosity of the Jesus of the Three Hours. The Church has to let go of all it has ever known and claimed, so that instead of trying to be the olympian torchbearer for humankind, it starts to live a true Christ life, for a new age, a new consciousness.

Gentleness is the key, with ourselves, with others. There is to be no berating, no violence, only gentleness. Yet we must be persistent too, though the way feel harsh and useless and full of misgivings. For sacred space will open up before us, and that is all that we are longing for, a space in which we can expand far beyond what we perceive ourselves to be. In the middle of the darkness, when all words fail, we live in the heart of God's presence, and it is there that the fruits of the Spirit start to ripen, the fruits that Paul wrote of: love, joy, peace, patience, kindness, goodness, trustfulness, gentleness (that word again!), and self-control.

LETTER THIRTY-ONE
Epiphany 2004

"Got him!" they said about Saddam Hussein. Oh dear! What a drab television shaped utterance which somehow encapsulated the miseries of our present world: dark words to a dark world that is getting darker. That profound biblical word 'tribulation' describes what is truly upon us. Judgments pile on top of judgments. At least, I suppose, the words and deeds of politicians, at home and abroad, are more exposed than ever before. The world is darker because of all those who want their views to be the only ones that count, their way the only way, whatever the cost. And the 'truth that will set us free' is far from us.

At Epiphany we recall the bringing of gifts into a dark world, so that joy may be known. The most extraordinary gift which the so-called wise ones bring is not the presents but themselves, for they have endured a long journey, with all its risks and dangers. They have left behind their everyday lives and their secure routines, and they have travelled into the unknown, keeping going day after day with all the discomfort and monotony.

For what? Do we see the paradox of uncertainty as to what they will discover, yet sure in their hearts that this journey is more important than anything else in their lives? Wise ones are those who know that they do not know the answers, despite all their knowledge and thirst for knowledge. The more they know, the less they are sure. As they move further and further from those who give them power and respect, they become nothing. They are like the Christmas card silhouettes, their individuality blacked out. They do not move as much by the compass of a star as by their own inner intuition and intent. Only so could they be prepared for the one bright star in a dark sky. And they see the mystery, in an instant, and are changed for ever. The story has it that "they returned to their own country another way."

It was the one big throw of their lives, as is ours in the prayer to which we are committed. In bringing the gift of ourselves beneath all the surfaces of our lives, we simply keep on journeying in prayer for long enough to allow things to change in us. We have to take the time because we have, little by little, to stop praying in our old familiar ways, which in time solidify as fixed patterns, repeated words, comfortable idols. Wise ones teach that 'real prayer begins when you stop praying.' Then the real journey begins, 'another way', and everything becomes prayer, guided by that inner star, clear even if we do not see every detail of the way before us.

The real journey for Annette began when she found herself moved out of all that was familiar and into a night place where all that she could say was, "Here I am." Stripped and shorn, it was her only gift, but it was her best gift. "Here I am" means, though it doesn't feel like it, "I am nearer than when I first believed." Like the Wise ones she feels helpless, but the only possibility we have of keeping the star in view is to travel in the dark. There is no choice, and all we can do is to choose to have no choice. It is the paradox at the heart of prayer.

I have lived in mining communities where 'getting on with it' is the terrible phrase I have heard widows repeat in family after family after the men they love have died down there in the pit, in the dark which they now share. Someone has died down there; something has died in here. All is dark, all the familiar landmarks have gone. All they have is uncertainty, and they have to live with that. "Here I am." You just have to get on with it.

To decide to live with the uncertainties of paradox, to choose to have no choice, is to flick the switch on a set of points and to follow a different track. And there is no going back.

At times you stop. And you sense a joy in the darkness. It is ridiculous but it is true. It is what the Three Hours is all about. It is to be like the Jesus who chose to have no choice, when he stopped teaching and healing and became passive. To use the title of W. H. Vanstone's book, he grew in 'the stature of waiting'. He handed himself over to helplessness and allowed to happen what was to happen, guided in the darkness by his own inner star – and even that was obscured towards the end, in those final hours when the whole world becomes night.

We are not Jesus, but we are called to accompany him, to 'be there', sitting in silence, without words, as helpless as we are by the bedside of someone whom we dearly love who is dying. "Here I am." It is my best prayer. It is my only prayer. It is the gift of the whole of me. It goes back to Exodus, to Moses, and to the God who says, I am who I am…I am has sent me to you. And it is a refrain through the Gospel of John: I am.

To be 'lost in prayer' is a good way of saying it. I remember a woman who left a prayer group because it seemed to her as she looked at the rest of us that we were 'away', better at it than she was. How little she knew! It was no seventh heaven, we were simply lost. We were not able to find our way, we were 'being there' and not very well either.

Jesus hands himself over to the darkness, not knowing, to 'save the world'. It is a paradox again. Paradox is ultimately at the heart of everything: having no power, yet having the power to save; giving up everything and yet being given everything; being lost and being found at the very moment of total lostness; everything we have known in prayer disappearing, even being ravaged, and in this absence the gift of presence; to become the darkness in order to save the world from its darkness; enduring the nothing-ness in order to find everything we dared to hope for; failing in order to succeed; emptied and in the moment of emptiness to be filled; choosing not to have a choice in order to be set free. "I'm dying to live." It's ridiculous, it's laughable, it's joy. But in living the dark mystery you come to know that it is all true.

"Got him!" is only the beginning of sorrows. In these times we are called, as people who want to pray, to live more deeply in the darkness that we may come to set free the star-lights of joy for others and for ourselves, whatever they are, whenever they appear, even if we do not know it. We shall know hereafter.

CONTRIBUTIONS
FROM MEMBERS

ONE

There is the brokenness, with panic, that *breaks down* to unresolved despair and repressed anger. There is also the brokenness, with letting go, that *breaks through* to resolution and transcendence.

It was 1968, a year of upheaval by young people. A number of hard things had come together in my life. My beloved father had died, my mother, for a long time deeply distressed, had been certified 'mad', our first child had been born amid scary complications, and, after 'taking off' with spirituality and politics under John Fenton and the Beatles, I had crashed into the 'brick wall' and the 'riot police' of the Church of England high up in a West Yorkshire moorland parish. I was very tired, then caught flu, followed by a depression, panic, and 'madness'. Broken, I had no sense of pain resolved.

By 1982 I had learned to cry again, for the first time since childhood, for my father and my mother, and to *breathe through* some of the panic. Then a number of hard things came again. Both my mother and my wife's mother died in a moment, within two days of each other. I was working ecumenically at the time, with abrasive dissent about leadership and spirituality, and meeting the 'brick walls' of three 'churches of England'.

Nights without sleep struggling to escape from the pit of the dead hour of three in the morning gave way to a waking dream. I am sitting, in desperation, on the edge of the bed. I am *tottering over* and *falling down*. I am *falling* for ever into the deepest darkest *void*. I am surprised that there is no panic. I become aware, imperceptibly, that I am being *caught*, and lowered to rest (like the way they used to teach us to catch the hard cricket ball in the school yard). I wait. I become aware, again imperceptibly, that I am being *raised up*. After an *eternal moment*, I *come awake* on the edge of the bed, my legs spring up and round, and I have one of those 'best nights for ages'.

Something had happened. Shifted? Deepened? I thought no more about it until, using the formal prayers of the Church, I found myself aware, in a very new way, of *who* it was that I was addressing: Almighty and Eternal God, and Father...If I were to use other metaphors, I was addressing *Kindly Darkest Pit, Eternal Embrace waiting for me within Depth of Void*.

I came, in prayer, to *rest* in *silence*, in this awareness of any one of my dark, hard, hurt places. I came to see movement out as taking *a risk*, approaching *the edge*, to *rest* again in the darkness and the hurt. I was *led* to take up ministry in Granby/Toxteth, often described as an 'open prison', the dark holy place of the riots of 1981, the home of a criminalized community. It is also the same community in which, in 1943, I was born, *the first time*.

> No it is not to despair that you bring me, but to humility. For true humility is, in a way, a very real despair, despair of myself, in order that I may hope entirely in You. What man can bear to fall into such darkness?
>
> THOMAS MERTON, *Thoughts in Solitude*

ROBERT GALLAGHER
Vicar of the Parish of St Margaret of Antioch, Toxteth, Liverpool 8 since 1990.

TWO

Words fail me.

This will be a surprise to anyone who knows me. I was brought up the confident eldest of six girls, steeped in Anglican liturgy and Socialist rhetoric, vaccinated, as my mother insists, with a long-playing gramophone needle (a what?)

And I have lost faith in words. I can still do it, still conduct Morning Prayer or other liturgies, preaching or praying aloud, using the names of God, Jesus, and Spirit. I can do this because *these* words in *these* settings encircle the gathered community and comfort the faint-hearted and suffering. They are our code, our passport to meaning.

But only a passport. The words are not the meanings themselves, and in so many liturgies I find words obscuring meanings and not illuminating them. Increasingly I find meaning in things I can touch, see, hear, taste, and smell. I make things all the time for people I know and people I don't know: earrings for a niece's birthday, a jumper and a teddy bear for a Romanian child's 'shoebox' gift, a quilt to raffle for a local hospice. Even better, I find meaning in teaching other people to make things.

At the local primary school we made four seasonal banners. The summer banner, a beautiful seaside scene made by six-year-olds, has moved recently. I told the children during assembly that one of our church ladies is very ill, and the one thing she wants to do is to get to the sea. We don't know if she'll be able to, but meanwhile the school has sent the sea to Margaret. The huge banner now adorns her living room door. Just think of the meanings there are in this gift, at this moment for Margaret, and, at some point in their future perhaps, for the children.

I open an unexpected package. My friend in Scotland has sent me a necklace which 'belongs round my neck'. As well as wearing it, I shall be wearing her love. All of us are flesh and blood, and the meanings we remember and treasure are those we experience with our senses. When words fail me, and they have, mostly, a homemade card and gift will say something more profound than anything I can ever say. I told the children at school about making cards out of magazine scraps and sending them to say, 'I care'. When I was in hospital I got 140 cards from them!

If there is any faith to be found or sustained, I find it in these things – the village ladies who bake cakes and make coffee to raise money for a cow and calf to be bought for villagers in Kosovo whom they will never meet, and who knit for Oxfam week after week. (Their own children and grandchildren find home knitting uncool. I wonder where they will find *their* meanings.)

Such crafting and giving is so easily derided. There are so many more important things that we could be doing. But the world of paid work has firmly shut its door against me. I could paper a room with letters from church-based organizations telling me of my undoubted gifts and their certainty that the Holy Spirit will find the right place for me (but not with them). I have wondered if I must be one of those to be "laid aside for you", in the words of the prayer in the Methodist Covenant Service. I expect you can understand how words have failed me.

At divinity school in Canada I entered some of my hymns as an untaught course paper. A leading homiletics teacher, Professor Paul Wilson, wanted to assess them on paper. I insisted on a hymn-singing so that he could judge the results. One of those who joined in said that for the first time ever a hymn had made him realize that his anger could be godly. Most hymns had asked him to leave his righteous indignation at the door. Even a hymn is only words until you have sung it in company and found your emotions and intellect stirred.

At the same time an artist entered a huge tapestry for her Ph.D at the Ontario Institute for Studies in Education. The professors wanted a paper explaining it. She refused. "It explains itself," she said. They saw the point, and she got her Ph.D.

Will our children be educated by SATS or by singing in a choir or banging a drum? That's the current debate in education. What makes us human, how do we pray and to whom do we pray? If you have an hour or two I could explain my complicated and endless train of thought through the language of theology, anthropology, and social psychology. Or I could make you a cup of tea and show you how to paint glass, make you some earrings, or knit you a woolly hat. Which of these will make you feel that prayer has been offered? How will prayers for earthquake victims in Algeria translate into shelter, clean water, food, and rebuilding? Is there after all any prayer that is not dark prayer?

I do not run away from these questions. While my hands are busy my mind is always swarming with them. But I do what I can, I make what I can, and in the small and beautiful gift hope that you find some of the questions in your own mind answered.

ANNA BRIGGS
is an artist living in Cambridgeshire where she is a team member of a local ecumenical project. She made the clown angel wallhanging for the annual competition at Clowns Café in Cambridge, and then realized that she had made a picture of herself.

She now clowns as Magenta and has one more ambition — to join the Clown Doctors (Theodora Trust) and work with children in a hospital.

THREE

'Dark prayer': I don't recall when I first came across the phrase, the name, the term. It was in any case a long time ago. Perhaps I had intimations of what it was, without knowing what it might be called. When David Wood wrote about it, I immediately knew to what he was referring. How, I'm not sure, for I doubt that 'dark prayer' can be communicated as a defined package. Suffice it to say that I think it can appear under different forms in potentially unlimited different circumstances.

Further back, some years before I realized all this, I was afflicted, and I wrote a poem that began:

In the end
the very smell of life
of death
is gone.
The wind has carried
all the cinder-seeds away.
The stake your pain-hot body charred:
a shrivelled stump,
a pimple on the earth.

Long and low and endless
is the whining of the void.
The life you sang
is jammed by no sound
pierced into my mind.
This crucifixion
dark and deep and timeless is...

For years, when I felt in a dark mood, I would recite this poem and persuade myself I was praying. But I've come to think that doing so was to rehearse a pattern of distress dressed up in a pretence of aesthetic dignity. I look at the Isenheim altarpiece in somewhat the same way – also, photographic images of desolation, whether from poverty, disease, or war. In it all I could observe myself gesturing, posing. It all aspires to become prayer, but in this form it may be no more than increasing self-awareness.

Again, from adolescence on, I imbibed 'right' ways to pray 'properly', and, during ordination training, that none was more right and proper than contemplative prayer. To be able to 'do' it was an accomplishment highly to be desired. Teachers of contemplation were to be prized "more than much fine gold". So, in 1985, when I witnessed David Wood play the part of Lo-ammi, the child of Gomer and Hosea (whose untranslatable name, usually rendered 'Not my people', resonates, according to Walter Hollenweger, most closely with the name 'Auschwitz') – and I do not remember having seen a more complete representation of crumpled, imploded, unborn man – I conceived a notion that this was how it's done. Concentrated layers of intensity are piled into the heart. You must show your love by trying harder to feel the pain more deeply. And it was only more romantic self-preoccupation, this time of the angst-filled contemplative.

Or again, I volunteered for a course that included 'plunging' into London with £1 to last 45 hours. Afterwards I was pleased I'd used my wits to get through without suffering any discomforts. Only later did I acknowledge that I'd done so by determining not to be faced with anything of which I might be afraid. I aimed to 'identify' and 'be in solidarity with' the homeless and vulnerable, but suffering was absolutely not on my agenda.

David invited me to join the Community of the Three Hours. I was at once delighted, flattered, to be asked (I must be on the right lines), and unnerved, for other insufficiencies that I'd managed to keep from myself would now be exposed to awareness. Despite David's assurances that there were no standards to be met and that all that was needed was the willingness to present oneself to unstructuredness for a period of time, I nonetheless knew that I wasn't up to the 'job'. Without props I would simply not be able to be faithful in 'dark prayer'. The challenge to be 'vigilant' during the 'Long Watch' had become an issue of 'moral fibre', a silent version of 'muscular Christianity'.

I very quickly submitted to feelings of unworthiness and treating myself as an also-ran. I 'had' to have books of prayer, or an Office to read, or people and situations for which to intercede, or a project to think about. And I decided I couldn't spare more than half the three hours, if that. Within that period patches of mental inactivity agitated my nerves. I began to use David's twice-yearly letters as if they were sacred texts, the meditative reading of which legitimated my not facing the beckoning void. The darkness of dark prayer was proving uncomfortable to the point of profound demoralisation.

But I could not get away from the sense of presence in this absence of peace – and the sense of being a guest, that it was not for me to serve, but to allow myself to be served whatever would be dished up. Friday at noon began to present a double allure: the one, dark matter cruising the void within and promising to overwhelm me, the other, an invitation to rest at the cross, a call drawing me closer to its source.

In time I began to cease resisting the nodding off that almost inevitably occurred after about half an hour. The invitation nowhere forbade the surfacing of fatigue that, detecting space and stillness asking to be filled, is eager to oblige. I began, too, gradually to recognize other features of the interior landscape. Sometimes moments of unsolicited illumination occur, in which I find my head and my whole body as if possessed by space, with brilliant sunshine briefly appearing through an otherwise overcast sky. Sometimes, too, I find myself as if thrown into the immediate presence of the crucified. No longer at the back of the crowd, I know I am seen in my wholeness, and thanked.

Mostly, though, the long watch is just that: long. About half way through my voices begin to insist that I am doing nothing useful here: there are more pressing ways of filling my time. There is no arguing with them; I just have to carry on, though by now usually feeling myself to be a liability at the cross. George Herbert's line from the poem 'Evensong' is a useful resource at this point: "Yet still thou goest on." It refers to God's patience with human shortfalling. The crucified have no choice; they will be staying for the duration, and whether or not I feel a liability is absolutely not the issue.

Not infrequently there may be some easing of burdens near the end of the vigil. At this time I have come to feel the truth of the Sabbath. It is a gift. God commands Sabbath observance, but observance merely prepares the ground for the gift of incommensurable space and conviction of well-being. It is at this level that Friday has come to be the fulcrum on which each week is balanced: behind the meal that binds people into fellowship and love, and behind the Christian celebration of Christ's resurrection is the cross which is the axis on which time spins. To attend to the creation that suffers there is to know something of love's achievement. I am grateful to have been invited, and I realize that many others have not yet known the blessing. I need now to enact the invitation that is entrusted to me.

DOUG CONSTABLE
Music has always been influential. Ordained in 1965. Contributed to the widespread uprootedness and confusion of the 1960s. Through illness knows the territory of being carried where one would rather not go. Since shortly after ordination has been a composer of songs, anthems, and most recently a collection of hymns, People Making Peace.

FOUR

God on the Edge of the Frame:
Dark Prayer through Film's Eye

In mining deeper and deeper seams of truth David Wood is frequently at a loss for words. 'Poor talkative Christianity' is not much good when you are at the coal face where the slightest noise can bring the one remaining prop crashing down. I am therefore struck by how cinematic he often is. In the aftermath of the destruction of the Twin Towers on 11 September 2001 he challenges those who struggle to force God 'into the frame'. This is your movie, God, and you refuse to star in it. Superman, Spiderman, the X-men and Neo (*The Matrix*) all do it better than you. It's that old habit-forming need for a *Deus ex machina* coming to the rescue, an idea which owes more to ancient Greece than to anything the New Testament teaches us. What would getting into the frame consist of spiritually? I am reminded of the little boy who asks his father if God is everywhere. "Yes, son, of course he is." "Is he in this room, Dad?" "Yes." "In this empty cup?" "Er, yes." And with his hand triumphantly swooping over the cup the boy cries, "Got him!"

You've been framed? The One in whom we live and move and have our being is far too wily for that. Oh no you don't. I am what I am. I shall be who I shall be.

Until recently, if we wanted the fuller picture we had to visit the cinema. Before the advent of widescreens, television always had to pan and scan, or, more likely, show us only the central part of the image. Anything peripheral was excluded from our view. Cary Grant in *To Catch a Thief* boards a bus. Sitting on the back seat he looks sideways to a fellow traveller with a birdcage on her lap. Then he glances in the other direction. The passenger is Alfred Hitchcock, the director of the film, making his usual fleeting appearance. On television we never got to see Hitchcock. The 4:3 'aspect ratio' prevented it. The film's creator is on the edge of the picture – like God. Dietrich Bonhoeffer speaks of a God who allows himself to be edged out of the world and on to a cross because that is the only way in which we can be challenged to participate in the sufferings of God in the life of the world. (*Letters and Papers from Prison*)

"Preach the Gospel and if necessary use words." The Community of the Three Hours is to praying what Francis of Assisi is to evangelism. It is economical with its use of language. When praying, Teresa of Avila managed to limit herself to two words, Our Father. Words can get in the way, be a smokescreen. Prayer is not about informing the Creator as to what is happening in creation. We are not praying so that God can hear but so that *we* begin to hear and attend to the silence of God. In the history of film, that highly formative first quarter century of its existence was made up of silent movies. In them there is "neither speech nor language yet their sound is gone out into all lands." (Psalm 19) Words were all but superfluous and cinema was then a truly international language. One of the great pioneering directors, D. W. Griffith, who filmed such movies as *Birth of a Nation* and *Intolerance*, described his task: "Above all, I am trying to make you *see*." Only if we abandon all presuppositions in praying can there be any possibility of the 'ray of divine darkness', to use Dionysius the Areopagite's telling phrase (*Mystical Theology*), illuminating our souls with a transforming perception. We need to practise seeing. Words do not enter the equation. If the coming of talkies ruined the career of many a player, we might well add, and also many a pray-er. God is there in any picture, but is usually first recognized out of the corner of our eye and not (using another image David Wood employs) in close-up. Who could bear such reality? When close-ups were first introduced into films, audiences were terrified and ran out of the cinemas screaming. I can sympathise. It was overwhelming enough an experience when I saw an IMAX film of a Rolling Stones concert. Mick Jagger's lips ten storeys high is an awesome sight.

So consider, then, who on this side of heaven could come close up to their Maker and survive the experience? Jacob, in the story in the Book of Genesis, managed to do so, but remember that the encounter begins in darkness, and having wrestled all night he still does not recognize, even at daybreak, that his sparring partner, the mysterious stranger, is God. Jacob is given a new name, 'Israel', which can mean one who struggles with God as well as someone who is protected by God. He is in fear and trembling because after twenty years he is coming home to face the brother whom he has cheated. His relationship with him is as dislocated as is his hip in the struggle. For in that darkness he is facing up to himself and in so doing discovers that God is in that place. With all the benefits that hindsight can bring, he says, "And I never knew it."

I never knew it because I was foolish, I had false expectations, I am so tunnel-visioned, I was too busy concentrating on my half-nelsons. Or, worse still, if I had known who I was contending with, the experience might well have killed me.

David Wood is warning those who want to go on dates with God to be sure they know what they are looking for. It is a fearful thing to fall into the hands of the living God. If we did, we might have to change our ways! Jacob does – but only after he has encountered the darkness and the stranger in the darkness.

In the film *Bruce Almighty* Jim Carrey rails against God for being the only one who isn't doing his job properly. That leads to his being landed with the onerous position himself. Answering millions of prayers each day turns out not to be much fun.

The Community of the Three Hours is predicated on an indecisive struggling with the God whose absence, when it isn't inducing rage and despair, can make the heart grow fonder. Many of us, including some of our most vociferous atheists, are like Jacob. They cannot leave God alone, demanding answers about who God is. We can appear victorious in our domestication or dismissal of God, only to find we have done the equivalent of shooting ourselves in the hip, unable to live with or without God. *Fight Club* is a remarkable movie where the protagonist, Edward Norton, arouses himself and others from emotional torpor by fighting, only to discover that the battle going on is not with Brad Pitt but with a self alienated from reality.

"Our passion is the presence of God in us, in our story. When for any reason we give up on ourselves, we fragment the passion." (Sister Grace Myerjack, quoted in Peter B. Price, *Playing the Blue Note: Journeying in Hope*) So whether fighting all night or staying with the darkness and its distractions, truly God was in this place and we did not know it – at the time.

David Wood suggests that our lives are but split-second exposures to the Light. "We are aware of ourselves only as a single frame in a long film about which we know nothing." But which frame do we want to be, and in which film? There are moments in films, as in prayer, that are as ikons. There is Gene Kelly *Singing in the Rain* with its extravagant joy and love. There is the lighting of a match in *Lawrence of Arabia* which crosscuts to the rising of the desert's greatest light. There is Marilyn Monroe's skirt being blown carefree up above her legs in *The Seven Year Itch*. All these images require more than a single frame for there has to be movement for us to be aware of them. But a still can often convey the essence of an entire scene or even a whole story. It pleads to capture the passing moment. Praying where words fail often involves fastening on a still moment, on one image that speaks for a million other moments.

> That was the real world; I have touched it once
> And now shall know it always.
>
> EDWIN MUIR
> from 'The Labyrinth', *Selected Poems*

Dark prayer does not know what is on the rest of the film. Hollywood likes closure, the happy ending. But life is rather more uncertain than that, more tentative, more like the parables of Jesus. Did the elder brother (in the parable of the Prodigal Son) accept his father's invitation to come inside and eat the fatted calf? Perhaps he stayed outside, preferring to luxuriate in his favourite bad mood. This uncertainty about how things end up can be deeply disturbing – or funny. In *The Purple Rose of Cairo*, directed by Woody Allen, one of the characters decides to step out of the film that is playing, leaving everyone else on the screen in turmoil. "If life's a lousy picture," suggest Roger McGough, "why not leave before the end?" (the title of a poem in *Watchwords*). Or rather, by leaving life as it is now the end will be transformed. Richard Rohr, quoted in Letter Twenty, says, in *Radical Grace* that Gospel people don't need to hold on to anything. They will make a difference in the world precisely because they don't feel that need to behave that way.

The uselessness of prayer is a case in point. Hanging around for three hours may not be everybody's idea of a good Friday, but it is an extravagant gesture, responding to God's munificence in the face of an adverse world. It reminds us whose world it is. And in silence there are incredible things actually going on. There are such moments in the films of Andrei Tarkovsky (*Solaris, Andrei Rublev*) where the cinematographer holds our gaze and meditates on what is being seen. The shot judges us as much as we judge it. What are you seeing? How long can you hold on to this? Imperceptibly in Michelangelo Antonioni's *The Passenger* and *L'Avventura* there are certain movements where the camera silently tracks back to reveal a larger picture. All it requires is that we keep faith in the process. A touchstone for the work of director Frank Capra were some words of Fra Giovanni, "There is a radiance and glory in the darkness, could we but see, and to see we have only to look. I beseech you to look!" (Jeanine Basinger, *The It's a Wonderful Life Book*)

The darkness and the light are both alike to God, says the Psalmist. But not to us. Darkness conceals things. It may frighten us. Yet it is an old familiar friend. Without it there would be no contrasts, shade, or contours. During an average length movie we subliminally see more than twenty-five minutes of blackness, the frames between the twenty-four images per second that reel past our eyes. Motion pictures would be impossible without those dark bits in between the changing images. The frame bars are a pause for thought before progressing to the next sequence of narrative. David Wood reminds us that Buddhists pray in order so to practise death that they may be fully alive. Dying to ego self requires us to plunge into a dark that is too deep for us, daring and daring to go further down. As Rowan Williams, referred to in Letter Twenty-Eight, has said, it needs patience and courage to enter the crucible of God where our desire may be transformed into God's desire. We need a lot of practice. Fred Astaire insisted on thirty takes for one dance routine in *Funny Face*. He was trying ever so hard for the perfect scene. Dark prayer also needs that kind of dedication, but alongside it there comes a point where we must learn to let go and let God. This may feel like hell, losing control. The Son is Godforsaken as he harrows hell. Jesus experiences being fatherless, that extremity of separation. It is a purging that is a prerequisite for new life. It can be a useful time, for examining those occasions of non-loving, not-being, when we have betrayed ourselves, and for asking Christ to befriend our treacherous self. A teenage boy was once asked what he thought Jesus was doing after the crucifixion. "I think on Friday he would have been spending time in hell looking for his friend Judas."

STEPHEN BROWN
from Ripley near Harrogate in Yorkshire has been involved since ordination with adult education and training in the Church locally, nationally, and internationally. He has now become a part-time parish priest so as to focus specially on 'training with films', working at the interface between spiritual development and the films millions know and love.

POSTSCRIPT

During the course of preparing this book for publication early in 2004, Jim Cotter wrote to David Wood with a couple of questions. Here are those questions, and David's response.

JIM WROTE:
I'd love a conversation with you about comparing the deliberate chosen entering into the darkness and the kind of unwilling plunge that happened to me in my 'brainsquall', my breakdown nearly ten years ago. Also this: I recognize in what you write some of the symptoms of the creative writing process, and I wonder if that is a sample of 'dark prayer' or if dark prayer is something uniquely different. My own inclination is to think the former, but I may be wrong (wouldn't be the first time).

DAVID REPLIED:
When I think of myself in relation to you and numerous others to whom the letters are addressed, I feel very much (as I say in one of the letters) like a prison visitor, on the outside of the experience of the darkness. I was not plunged into it against my will, against my *whole* being. I have not inhabited – not for long – that sense of lostness. But I do feel rescued, lifted up, forgiven out of a black hole into which I allowed myself to slide. In a way it is burn-out. You can see it coming, you know what you could do to prevent it, but somehow the momentum is too great, the will is too weak in the confusion.

It focuses inevitably around the breakdown of my first marriage. I remember writing to one of the family that I felt I had driven through too many red lights till I was saying to myself, "It's all too late, let it happen."

On the other hand there was (and is) behind it all a sense of compelling mystery, a destiny to fulfil or fail. For years I had been nursing this sense, this desire to form a community: not to be part of one, but to form it. I longed for people to be gathered together in some form of deeper prayer and spiritual life. When I was forty-six and away on a course, I had to write a stream-of-consciousness personal obituary, and I described myself as being at the centre of such a community when I died!

Well, I had lots of grand ideas about it all, encouraged in my fantasies by what other men and women were doing. With the collapse of my marriage, everything disappeared. I was hanging on, just taking the next step, starting all over again. And yet, and yet, I was led to stumble on into new beginnings, away from something that *I* wanted to start, into a new relationship with 'community', being led into something which others had started and was already growing. Out of nothing I have been re-shaped, but that sense of a destiny to fulfil has held good, and here I am, approaching my mid-seventies, living the vision in a deeply satisfying way, being carried through more than doing the carrying. I am also involved, locally and nationally, with the World Community for Christian Meditation, and I seem to move easily between it and the Community of the Three Hours, the one feeding the other. I don't quite know how all this has happened. God does not withdraw his promises, nor his gifts. It's stunning.

So I suppose that I knew dark prayer, waiting prayer, was the way through, the way on. I owed it everything. And I was drawn to explore this darkness more, which I could do only by being there. Encouraged by others, I wanted to encourage others in my turn, and like so many I was weary of all the pat answers and processes by which I had let myself down. There is a mystery here, unique to each and every one of us. We have to stay with it, address it, love it. I'm running out of words, but you will get the gist, I know. The darkness is the secret, not the light.

I love the phrase, 'symptoms of the creative writing process'. In many ways I feel I don't know much about it, but it is to do with the empty page and waiting for every part of yourself to come together on it. At school we studied some of Lamb's essays: the only bit I remember is of his sitting there "shedding tears of helpless despondency on the blank, unfinished paper". It's about trying to reach into meanings and never quite getting there. So yes, I am sure that there is a both/and in the letters, there is the tension of wanting to address and create something that is of vital importance, and at the same time of being addressed by something. Certainly in writing the letters I have drawn from far beyond my own experience, as using other people's words continually shows…

Two things are perhaps going on at the same time. Yes, I was driven by by my own needs, but also there is that which dwells in the seeds of my own being which is of the generosity of God and the desire to share every part of the Way with others. In Jesus as the Son we have nothing but generosity, only generosity, no driven needs. There is certainly driven need expressed in these letters (I wonder, is that sense of compulsion part of the creative writing process?), and I am not at all able to disentangle them from the generosity and the sharing. After all, I am both Jekyll and Hyde, both fallibly human and divine. Amen.

ACKNOWLEDGMENTS

I have many people to thank for what is written here, especially:

John Fenton, whose teaching, influence, and friendship from the earliest days of my entry into 'religion' and the life of faith have been profound.

The many hidden companions, the inspiration for these letters, whose example and responses have encouraged me to write just the next letter.

Francis Dewar, his single-minded courage in following his calling and taking just the next step, and his hawk-eye intelligence and unfailing loyalty. David Goodacre, for his sense of balance and his enduring friendship. I cannot think of either of these without the other.

Jim Cotter, a profound gratitude for guiding me through the process of preparing this book, and for such a comprehensive and scrupulous editing of the original letters. He has taken my somewhat peremptory and exclamatory style and skilfully eased it into a continuous narrative. It is one thing to write a letter every six months, quite another to bring them all together into a book.

Sheila, my wife, for whom I reserve my best thanks. Without her patience and recurring willingness to work with me, these letters would never have been typed up and seen the light of day.

Robert Gallagher, Anna Briggs, Doug Constable, and Stephen Brown, members of the Community of the Three Hours, for their particular responses to the letters. They are reproduced here with their permission.

More formally, I have quoted from the following writings and I am grateful for permission to include them where they are still in copyright. Every effort has been made to trace the source of some of the random extracts and if I have inadvertently breached copyright I apologize and will set this right in any future edition of this book.

Anon, *The Cloud of Unknowing*, John M. Watkins, 1956

Basinger, Jeanine, *The It's a Wonderful Life Book*, Wesleyan University Press, 1986

Bonhoeffer, Dietrich, *Letters and Papers from Prison*, SCM Press, 2001

Cassidy, Sheila, quoted in *The Tablet*

Cotter, Jim, *Prayer at Night*, Cairns Publications, 1988

Cotter, Jim, *Brainsquall*, Cairns Publications, 1997

Cotter, Jim, *Waymarks*, Cairns Publications, 2001

Crowther, May, quoted in *Prayer at Night*, op. cit.

The Dalai Lama, *The Good Heart*, Random House Group, 1996

De Mello, Anthony, *One Minute Wisdom*, Gujarat Sahitya Prakash, Publishers and Booksellers, PB no. 70, Anand (Gujarat) 388 001, India

De Mello, Anthony, *The Song of the Bird*, published as previous entry

De Mello, Anthony, *The Prayer of the Frog*, published as previous entry

Dewar, Francis, *Called or Collared*, SPCK, 1991

Dickinson, Emily, *Everyman's Poetry*, J. M. Dent, Orion Publishing Group, 2001

Dillard, Annie, *Pilgrim at Tinker Creek*, Harper Perennial, 1998

Dionysius the Areopagite, *Mystical Theology*, Bantam Press, 1992

Ecclestone, Alan, *The Night Sky of the Lord*, DLT, 1980. By permission of Martin Ecclestone

Ecclestone, Alan, quotation from an unpublished address, reproduced by permission of Martin Ecclestone

Fenton, John, quoted from an address, 'Re-inventing the Church', 1997

Fox, Matthew, *Breakthrough: Meister Eckhart's Creation Spirituality*, Image Books, Doubleday, 1991, reproduced by permission of Random House Inc., USA

Griffiths, Bede, *A New Vision of Reality*, Harper Collins, 1992

Hammarskjøld, Dag, *Markings*, Faber, 1966

Hewitt, Catherine, 'Disillusionment', an unpublished poem, and I have not been able to trace its source formally to ask for permission

Hillesum, Etty, *Etty – A Diary 1941–43*, Jonathan Cape, 1983, by permission of the Random House Group

John of the Cross, St, *Collected Works*, Burns Oates Ltd, 1964

Jones, Rufus H., *The Radiant Life*, publishing details not traced

Julian of Norwich, *Enfolded in Love*, DLT, 1980

Kuyama, Kusuke, *Three Mile an Hour God*, SCM Press, 1979

Mary Clare, Mother, *Encountering the Depths*, SLG Press, 1993

Nash, Wanda, *A Fable for Our Time*, Christians Aware, 2002

McGough, Roger, *Watchwords*, Jonathan Cape, 1969

Muir, Edwin, 'The Labyrinth', *Selected Poems*, Faber and Faber, 1965

Myerjack, Sister Grace, quoted in Peter B. Price, *Playing the Blue Note: Journeying in Hope*, SPCK, 2002

Nouwen, Henri J. M., *Finding My Way Home*, DLT, 2001

Peel, David, *Ordinary Glory*, unpublished, Newcastle University

Rohr, Richard, *Radical Grace*, St Antony Messenger Press, Cincinnati

Rutter, Lizbet, Personal communication

Sacks, Oliver, *A Leg to Stand On*, Summit Books, 1984

Simonov, Konstantin, 'Wait for me', quoted in John McCarthy and Jill Morrell, *Some Other Rainbow*, Bantam Press and Random House, 1993

Society of the Precious Blood, Burnham Abbey, Lake End Road, Taplow, Maidenhead, Berkshire

Teilhard de Chardin, P., *The Hymn of the Universe*, Harper Collins, 1970

Thomas, R. S., *Counterpoint*, Bloodaxe Books, 1990

Tillich, Paul, 'Waiting', *The Shaking of the Foundations*, SCM Press, 1949

Verney, Stephen, source unknown

Wilkinson, Frances, for her poem and letter

A NOTE ON TREES

How many trees have been used to publish this book? Well, only the pulp is used, which comes from the trimmings: the trunks are used for furniture. A commercially grown softwood tree produces, on average, about one-sixth of a ton of pulp. Since this book has used about one ton, it has needed the pulp of six trees to produce it. But by weight it has needed only three-quarters of one tree. So Cairns Publications is donating the wherewithal for the planting of two trees, in gratitude and recompense.